BOOK 1
Part One
CREATION

If you are reading this book then you exist. You can see and feel and think. You are part of the human race, which is part of the world we live in, which is part of the Universe we live in, which is part of . . .?

The first part of this book centres around the theme of Creation and in it we tackle some of the big questions in life. Questions like . . .

Who am I?
What am I like?
What is the Universe?
How did we get it?
Is there a God?
If there is – what is God?
If God exists can we know him, her, it?
Is there a purpose and a plan for my life?

Yourself

WHO ARE YOU?

How would you describe yourself? If you were writing to someone who had never met you but who wanted to be a friend, what would you consider it important to mention about yourself? You would probably begin with a physical description. This, of course, is easy. You are either tall, medium height or short, thin, average weight or overweight. Your eyes are either green, blue, brown or grey and your hair could be anything from purple to silver depending on taste!

Do you leap to conclusions when you look at people? You might say, from simply looking at someone, that they are boring, rich or lonely but you could only be sure that you were right if you took the time to get to know them personally. It is just possible that old ladies enjoy break dancing and that someone who looks like a businessman goes stock car racing – unlikely but possible!

When we classify a number of people according to their appearance, their nationality or their behaviour we call this *stereotyping*. Some adults stereotype all young people as good for nothing thugs because they only look at the physical appearance. Or perhaps they have known one youth who was a vandal and that is enough to convince them that every youth is the same. This attitude is one of *prejudice*.

How do we see ourselves? And how would we like other people to see us?

"...and Doris, there's a signed photo of yours truly winging it's way to you right now!"

LOOKING INSIDE

It is obvious that physical appearances are not enough to give us a true picture of what a person is like. The human personality is highly complex and to get to know someone we have to spend time with them, discovering what their behaviour and attitudes are like. Here is one very simple way of looking at these different aspects of ourselves:

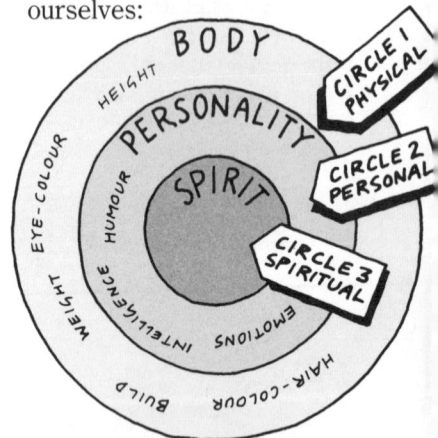

An important part of our personality belongs to circle 2 – our attitudes and our actions. What makes us think and act in the way we do? Why do some people think study is a good thing and others see it as a necessary evil until they leave school? What about our temperament? Why are some people always miserable and others always cheerful? Why are some quick-tempered and others quiet-spirited? We inherit many of our characteristics from our parents, and our attitudes and our behaviour is also shaped by our experience of life.

Perhaps the most powerful of all the influences upon us is the atmosphere and environment of our home. At an early age we begin the learning process and what is learned either consciously or subconsciously in the first seven years or so will influence us to some degree for the rest of our lives.

DAVID AND THE ALSATIAN

When he was three years old, David walked into the kitchen and to his surprise found a big Alsatian dog. He tried to stroke him but the dog became aggressive and jumped at him, barking furiously. David started to cry.

His mother came to the rescue. She told him to be a big boy and to stop crying. Although David is now fifteen years old, he is still scared of Alsatians – although never admits it. In addition, he never allows himself to cry because from a very early age he learned that it is silly for boys to cry.

But David was able to find a way out. Because he was able to remember the incident with the dog and knew why he was afraid of Alsatians, this knowledge helped him to overcome the problem.

A lot of what we take in is done subconsciously, without us knowing it. Laws have now been passed to ban what is called *subliminal* advertising. Put simply, this is when an advert is flashed on the screen so fast that the eye does not focus although the brain registers it. For example, if the words, 'Attention men! For real muscle buy Adonis Miracle Mix' were flashed on the TV screen, so that next morning every eligible male between the ages of seventeen and forty was queueing at the local drugstore then they would have been persuaded subliminally. They would never even know it!

How many other things have influenced us and shaped our lives without our knowing it? You might think *your* opinions and beliefs are quite your own and that you have thought them out all by yourself. But psychologists tell us that we are influenced from our earliest years at every level by other people and by our environment.

But in spite of all this you *are* unique! There is no one quite like you living on planet earth. You may know someone who is similar to you in their personality or their looks, but no one is a duplicate. Your thoughts, your beliefs and even your fingerprints

Our characters are made up of many different elements: humour, aggression, obstinacy, and so on. Try cutting up different faces from a magazine and sticking them together like this one to show what you are like – or what you would rather be like.

WHAT SHAPES US?

- Opinions of those who bring us up in the home
- Experiences as a child
- Television, videos and the media
- Travel and education
- Friends and what they think of us
- Music and its message
- People we meet

TYPICAL! YOUNG PEOPLE. NO RESPECT, BUMPING INTO PEOPLE...

SILLY OLD FOOL. CAN'T EVEN WALK STRAIGHT

SORRY

SUDDENLY!

CRUMP!

AAAAH!

MEANWHILE

LET ME THROUGH, I'M A DOCTOR

WITHIN MINUTES

DA DA DA DA DA DA

EXCUSE ME, BUT I'M FROM THE 'DAILY NOISE'. CAN YOU TELL ME WHAT HAPPENED?

WELL, IF THIS YOUNG MAN HADN'T THOUGHT QUICKLY AND CALLED AN AMBULANCE, THAT GIRL COULD HAVE DIED.

THE DOCTOR HERE KNEW JUST WHAT TO DO. HE DIDN'T PANIC - HE SAVED HER LIFE

are different from those of other people. You are distinct.

THE SPIRITUAL DIMENSION

In the 'looking inside' section, we looked at a simple diagram of ourselves. Look at circle 3, labelled 'the spiritual dimension'. The spirit of men and women obviously cannot be seen and it is not so easily identifiable as our mental processes or our physical self. But the spiritual dimension is nevertheless a vital part of our whole existence. For just as:

● My physical body enables me to move and function . . .
● My personality enables me to love and learn, so . . .
● My spirit enables me to discover and experience what is greater than myself or the world.

This may all sound rather strange. Some people would prefer to call it a religious sensitivity, but whatever we call it, the spiritual side is that part of us which is not satisfied with the view that we are born for no reason, live for no particular purpose and then die and disappear for ever into nothing. Our spiritual activity is concerned with looking for meaning in life and beyond life and so we search for answers to the **big questions in life**.

Have you ever caught sight of yourself in front of a mirror, or perhaps you have lain awake at night and thought: 'Who am I?' or 'Why am I here?' or even 'Who made me?' Most people have to ask these questions at some time or another but it is easy to be persuaded by other people's opinions and especially the social climate of the day, rather than to find out for yourself and make up your own mind.

In the Victorian era, society expected people to be religious and most people were. But today we would be very surprised if 90 per cent of our class at school voluntarily turned up for church on a Sunday morning, for church is not 'the fashion' today. Often the attitude which comes across is that if you are under twenty years of age and you go to church regularly you must be some sort of religious freak!

Society can be religious or it can mock religion, but that does not make the issues of life and death and the possibility of a God any the less important. We need to find out for ourselves.

·F·O·L·L·O·W·U·P·

1. Draw a 'fan-club' profile of yourself like the one below, but put in your own personal information.

Name Clementine Legg
Age 21
Born 26.1.62
Occupation Actress
Height 5′ 6″ (metres)
Hair Blonde (at the moment)
Eyes Blue
Nationality American
Favourite subjects at school Art, Biology, History
Favourite Colour/s Green and purple
Favourite food Roast beef, hamburgers, curry and chips, blackcurrants (but not all at once)
Hobbies Singing, rock music, swimming, car mechanics, cats, dogs, sheep and gerbils, growing tomatoes
Personality Cheerful usually, can be bossy, shy when meeting new people
Likes People who don't pretend to be what they're not, old Postcards, the seaside
Dislikes Show-offs, tinned pears and cruelty to animals

Religion I think there's a God but I'm not sure what he's like
Ambitions To be happily married, write a book on growing tomatoes and start a home for ill-treated animals

2. Write a sentence explaining what is meant by these words:
○ subliminal
○ prejudice
○ subconscious
○ stereotype

3. Look at the comic strip. This is a story of how two people's prejudices about each other were broken down. What were their prejudices? In a few sentences, write a story (fact or fiction) about how one of *your* prejudices was broken down.

The Universe

HOW MANY STARS?

If you look out on a clear night you'll be able to see some 2,000 stars in the heavens. With a pair of strong binoculars about 100 times as many will be visible. Of course, the number increases with more powerful equipment. So while about 30,000 million suns are at present known to be in our galaxy, there are actually many more.

THE CENTRE OF THE UNIVERSE

If someone were to tell you that the Earth was at the centre of the universe and that everything else revolved around it, you would not take them very seriously. But there was a time when you could have been executed for believing otherwise. Up until the beginning of the seventeenth century, everyone still believed that the Earth was the centre of everything.

This theory was brought to its greatest expression by Ptolemy of Alexandria who lived from AD 120 to 180 and was the greatest astronomer of his time. On his theory, the Sun, Moon and all the planets revolved around the Earth in perfect circles and beyond them was a fixed sphere of stars which revolved once each day. Since everyone wanted the Earth to be at the centre of

Nicolaus Copernicus, the Polish astronomer. He sparked off a revolution in science by saying that the Sun, not the Earth, was at the centre of the Solar System.

Since the 1960s, manned and unmanned spacecraft have explored our nearest neighbours in space. This picture was taken on the surface of Mars on the afternoon of 6 September 1976. The largest rocks are about two feet across, and in the distance some hills catch the afternoon sun.

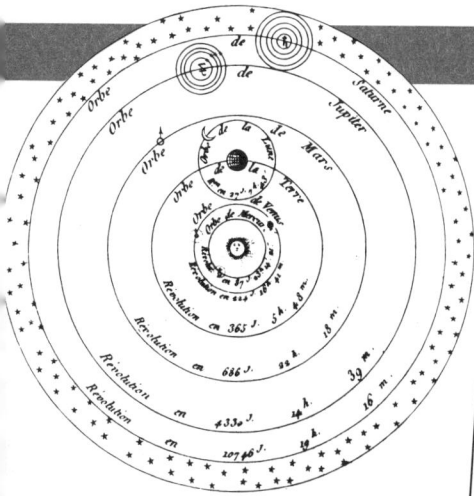

Caption (right of Did You Know box): Copernicus's view of the Universe. The Sun is at the centre, the planets orbit around it, and beyond Saturn are the stars.

DID YOU KNOW?

● Light travels at 186,000 miles per second. Some stars are so far away from us that their light takes 100,000 years to reach us. We are seeing them as they looked 100,000 years ago. And that is just stars from inside our galaxy. With powerful equipment you can see hundreds of other galaxies. Maybe what we see is what our galaxy was like that long ago?

● The fate of a photon. A photon is a ray of light born in the Sun. If it starts in the centre it could take 20,000 years to reach the outside (matter in the Sun is so dense). It would then take about eight minutes to travel across space, through our atmosphere and to the back of your eye. That's where its journey stops – dead.

● The Sun's diameter is about 864,000 miles. If If the Earth was the size of a table tennis ball, then the Sun would be about 13½ feet in diameter. Compared to the Sun, the Earth is tiny, and compared to the universe the Sun is a mere speck! But Earth is our home and it's probably the only planet you've visited! Small though it is, our planet is extremely complex and varied in its character.

the Solar System, Ptolemy's universe was accepted and no one challenged this view.

But eventually, in the mid-sixteenth century, a Polish clergyman called Nicolaus Copernicus realized that something was wrong. He published a book entitled: *De Revolutionibus Orbium Coelestium*, meaning, *Concerning the Revolutions of the Celestial Bodies*. In it he stated that the Sun, and not the Earth, was at the centre of the Solar System. But because this was contrary to the teachings of the Church, Copernicus (being a priest himself) withheld publication until the end of his life so that he would escape the reprimands of his fellow churchmen.

·F·O·L·L·O·W·U·P·

1. Do you think there could be life on other planets? Give reasons for saying yes or no.

2. Governments spend money on many different things – including space research. Which of the following do you think is more valuable? Put them in order of importance and say why.

● Space research programmes
● Education
● Health and Social Services
● Unemployment Benefits
● Nuclear defences
● Aid to World Poverty and Hunger
● Law and Order

3. In your opinion did Copernicus do the right thing by avoiding public abuse and waiting to publish his book or should he have printed it openly despite opposition?

4. We call the sort of pressure Copernicus faced *social* or *group* pressure. Give an example of group pressure in your community or school where people try to get you to conform in either your behaviour, your attitudes or your personal appearance.

5. Draw two columns, labelling one 'I agree' and the other 'I disagree'. Which column would you put the following widely-held attitudes and opinions in?

● Men should never cry
● Everyone should be treated fairly
● Murder is wrong
● If it's written in the newspaper it's true
● No one should steal from another person
● It isn't right to talk about someone behind their back
● Men of fifty shouldn't marry girls of eighteen
● Divorce is the best thing if two people don't get on
● People over twelve years of age shouldn't read the *Beano*

Spaceship Earth

The total area of the Earth has been calculated at 197 million square miles.

29% = land

71% = water

We live on a planet of incredible natural beauty . . .

- Of deserts and dunes
- Forests, fields and fjords
- Mountains, rocks, plains
- Oceans, rivers, streams, lagoons
- Caverns, chasms, canyons
- Volcanoes, valleys

We can either pollute or preserve our planet. Here are some of the ways we cause POLLUTION:

WE HAVE PROBED
THE EARTH,
EXCAVATED IT,
BURNED IT, RIPPED
THINGS FROM IT,
BURIED THINGS IN
IT... THAT DOES
NOT FIT MY
DEFINITION OF A
GOOD TENANT. IF
WE WERE HERE
ON A MONTH-TO-
MONTH BASIS, WE
WOULD HAVE BEEN
EVICTED LONG AGO.

ROSE ELIZABETH
BIRD, CHIEF
JUSTICE,
CALIFORNIA

- in the air

- on the land

- in the sea and in rivers

Here are some of the ways we cause PRESERVATION

- in the air

- on the land

- in the sea and in rivers

Can you put a name to each of these tree shapes? Choose between beech, oak, elm, scots pine and silver birch. Answers at the end of this unit.

A   B   C   D   E

Creatures great and small. The elephant, the largest land animal, has 40,000 muscles. The flea, on the other hand, has no muscles, but it is infested with mites, which can be seen under its scales in the close up.

We could spend all year learning about the intricate and fascinating world of animal life. The variety of life on our planet is overwhelming . . .

Unlike animals bacteria do not have organs, a heart, and eyes (for example), and yet they are living creatures. They are so small that we can only see them under a microscope. It is no use trying to measure this sort of life in metres, so scientists had to invent a new unit of measurement called the micron (one millionth of a metre). But even this was not sufficient for thorough investigation, so the electron microscope measures in Angstroms (which is one ten thousandth of a micron!) There is so much going on that we cannot see, feel or hear. But with the right equipment, it can be measured.

Can you put a name to each of these rivers? Choose between the Mississippi, Congo, Nile and Amazon. Answers at the end of this unit.

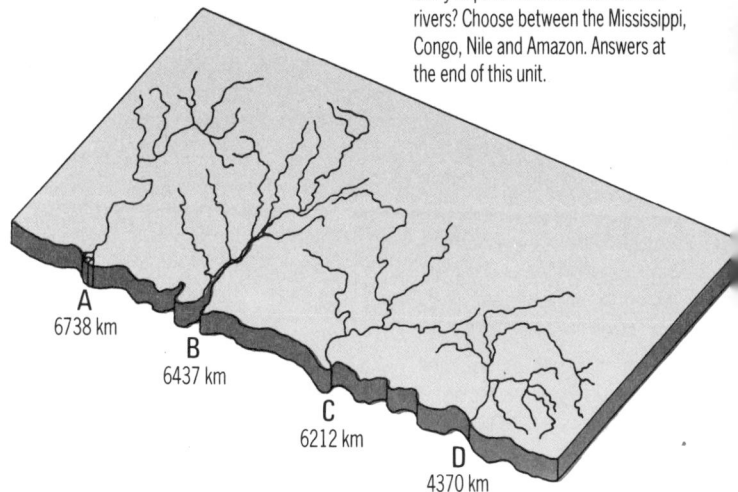

A
6738 km

B
6437 km

C
6212 km

D
4370 km

This was once a clean, busy canal. It has now become a rubbish tip. Pollution is one of the biggest problems facing humankind.

But how do you measure instinct and intelligence? Some forms of life amaze us with their abilities:

DID YOU KNOW?

● Bats have tiny eyes – so how do they manage to find and catch insects in the dark? Research scientists covered the eyes of some bats in their laboratory and then put them through an obstacle course of poles and ropes hanging from the ceiling. The blindfolds made no difference to their ability to fly. They flew around and between the poles with ease. It was obvious that they did not depend on their eyes at night. Yet when tiny plugs were put in their ears, the bats were almost helpless in the air, hitting the first poles they came to. Quite clearly they were using their ears to fly properly.

When electronic equipment was used, scientists were able to hear the sound of tiny pulses or sounds sent out by the bats which bounced off objects and came back. This is called echo-location, or finding direction by listening to echoes. A fraction of a second after the bat sends out a signal it receives an echo back. It is even able to interpret the echo in terms of distance and direction. In this way it can avoid obstacles and catch insects in mid air. A bat's senses are, in some ways, more accurate than the latest and most expensive radar systems that we have invented.

● Some birds travel thousands of miles to migrate in their search for food. The Arctic Tern is known to make an annual journey which is equivalent to one complete circumference of the equator (some 25,000 miles)

Answers to rivers quiz:
A Nile, B Amazon, C Mississippi, D Congo.

Answers to trees quiz:
A oak, B scots pine, C beech, D silver birch, E elm.

·F·O·L·L·O·W·U·P·

1. How many can you name?
○ Seas and oceans
○ Rivers in Britain
○ Countries in Europe
○ Forests and woods
○ Famous deserts in the world
Now get a map and add to your list!

2. Copy down the ways in which we pollute and preserve our environment using the headings: Air, Land and Sea/Rivers. In addition give an example of preservation or pollution in your area.

3. Which of the following do you think is the most intelligent creature, and why? Dog, dolphin, ostrich, pigeon, lion, ant.

4. Debate: attitudes to animals. Write a few lines saying why you agree or disagree with the following three statements:
○ Nobody should eat meat because it is cruel to kill animals just to feed ourselves.
○ There is nothing wrong with fox hunting.
○ We need to experiment on animals so that products can be tried out without hurting people.

The Human Race

If we think that the animal world is varied, take a look at the human race! In some ways, people have similarities with the animal world. We have instincts of survival, we can smell, taste, and feel. But in other ways we are very different – a horse does not read the paper, a rhinoceros does not go to school. Mankind is the most dangerous species on Earth, because to a large extent we have power over our environment . . .

HUMANS: GOOD
- Medical Science, skills of healing
- Fair hearing for those charged with offences
- Financial help and aid for the poor
- Technological advances mean better living standards
- Education for the majority and not the minority
- Laws prohibiting racial discrimination
- The right to vote
- Improvement in the rights of equality for women
- Care for the disabled

HUMANS: BAD
- Rapid increase in violent crime and murder
- Growth of divorce, broken homes, child abuse
- Exploitation of animal life: whales, seal skins, over-fishing
- More and more wars: Lebanon, Northern Ireland, Afghanistan
- Increase in unemployment: disillusioned youth
- Pollution of rivers, the sea, land and air
- Some eat too much, others die of starvation

People have walked on the moon but we can't solve the world's hunger. We have nuclear power enough to destroy the world, yet we can't destroy the hate that starts wars and builds weapons. Surgeons can transplant a human heart, but we can't transform it.

The human heart is capable of so much good. We save life sometimes at great personal risk. We take pity on someone in trouble or give to those less fortunate than ourselves. Yet the human heart is also capable of so much selfishness. We want money or power to show how great we are, or we can look for physical satisfaction at the expense of others.

MONEY, POWER AND SEX
It is not difficult to spot people who buy cars and houses and holidays or household equipment such as videos, not so much for their own sake or for personal

Whether your favourite is swimming, volleyball, snooker or whatever – sports are a way in which we can get a lot out of life.

enjoyment but so that they can impress their friends. Whoever the Joneses are, they are expensive to keep up with!

Most of us will have met or know of people who want power. This does not only apply to politicians! It can also happen in a family with a dominating brother, sister or parent. At school there are always those who want to bully and be looked up to.

The need for sexual relationships is well known and natural but when the main motivating factor is that of

German riot police prepare for a demonstration.

satisfying yourself without a permanent commitment to the other partner then the result can be disastrous. Both men and women are left heartbroken as the partner goes off in search of another to satisfy.

DO I MATTER?

Why do so many of us behave like this? Perhaps one of the reasons is that we are afraid that we don't matter, that we are insignificant and a nobody, so in order to feel better we try to be a somebody, whether it's by accumulating status or power over others or by using other people for our own ends.

This raises a very important question: Do we matter? Not just do I matter because I'm someone's son or daughter, partner or friend, but do I matter because I am *me*, a person? Is there any purpose for my life? Is the human race just an 'accident' of nature, or do we mean something to the one who created it? In other words, is there a God, a supernatural being, who had a purpose in creating you and me?

As you can imagine there are countless answers to this question. In the next chapter we will look at what different people think, and examine the evidence for ourselves.

Test Yourself

Do you see yourself as someone who has power over the things which affect your life? Choose between each of the following statements and then look up the scores at the bottom of the page to see how you did.

1a. Many of the unhappy things in people's lives are partly due to bad luck.
b. People's misfortunes result from the mistakes they make.

2a. No matter how hard you try some people just don't like you.
b. People who can't get others to like them don't understand how to get along with others.

3a. One of the major reasons why we have wars is because people don't speak up about what is wrong.
b. There will always be wars, no matter how hard people try to prevent them.

4a. Becoming a success is a matter of hard work, luck has little or nothing to do with it.
b. Getting a good job depends mainly on being in the right place at the right time.

5a. There is some good in everybody.
b. There are certain people who are just no good.

6a. Sometimes I can't understand how teachers arrive at the grades they give.
b. There is a direct connection between how hard I study and the grades I get.

HOW DID YOU SCORE?
For the following award a score of 2:
1b, 2b, 3a, 4a, 5b, 6b
For the following award a score of 0:
1a, 2a, 3b, 4b, 5a, 6a

SCORES
0–2. You do not see yourself as having much influence over the things which happen to you. It's probable that you think life gives you a rough deal and that other people have it in for you!
2–8. You are an interesting mixture. In certain things you are very confident of your ability to cope but in others you feel that you have no say in what happens to you.
8–10. You are probably at times overconfident of your abilities and opinions, this may result in others thinking you're a 'know it all'. However you think you have a good future in life and you take challenges in your stride.
12. You think you are going places – and you probably are!

F·O·L·L·O·W·U·P·
1. Choose one of the following to write about:
○ The most unselfish person I know.
○ The person I admire most.
2. Look again at the section above, **Money, power and sex**. When these are misused which do you dislike and why?

Creation and Evolution

This clay tablet was inscribed, 2,700 years ago, with a story of the world's creation. It comes from ancient Babylon. Ancient accounts of creation are strikingly different from the one found in the Bible.

So far we have been concerned with *what* we have in creation – and therefore we have had a potted look at Yourself, the Universe, the Earth, Animal Life and Creatures, and Mankind.

Now we are concerned with *how* we got it. At best we can only come up with intelligent theories and beliefs on the subject. After all, none of us was around at the time of the first living cell! A theory is a way of trying to explain certain facts. The facts are that we are all living human beings who can read this book. We are all individuals who have likes and dislikes. We live in a very complex environment of living things – minute and huge. We exist on a planet which in turn is only a tiny part of a massive Universe, which might possibly be only a minute part of the whole which we have no way of measuring. How then can we explain the existence of these things? How did the world, the Universe itself, begin? We are going to look at two theories which have different perspectives: creation and evolution.

THE CREATION OF THE UNIVERSE

The belief that God created the World or that God is the source of all life is expressed in many of the world's great religions.

IN THE JEWISH AND CHRISTIAN FAITHS God creates everything that is. In Muslim, Jewish and Christian faith creation is usually thought of as being what we call *ex nihilo*, which means that God created the Universe out of nothing that existed before. The opening verse of the Bible says:

'In the beginning, when God created the universe, the earth was formless and desolate. The raging ocean that covered everything was engulfed in total darkness, and the power of God was moving over the water. Then God commanded, "Let there be light" – and light appeared.'

IN THE MUSLIM FAITH Allah is the all-powerful one, the creator.

'He is Allah, besides whom there is no other god. He is the Sovereign Lord, The Holy One, the Giver of Peace, the Keeper of Faith; the Guardian, The Mighty One, the All-powerful, the Most High! Exalted be He above their idols! He is Allah, the Creator, the Originator, the Modeller. His are the gracious names. All that is in heaven and earth gives glory to Him. He is the Mighty, the Wise One'.

IN THE HINDU FAITH the first verse of the Isha Upanishad expresses the thought that at the heart of this world is the 'Unchanging Lord'.

'At the heart of this phenomenal world, within all its changing forms, dwells the unchanging Lord. So, go beyond the changing, and, enjoying the inner, cease to take for yourself what to others are riches.'

IN THE SIKH FAITH the beginning of Guru Nanak's hymn, from the Adi Granth, is recited by Sikhs every morning to express their faith.

'There exists but one God, who is called the True, the Creator, free from fear and hate, immortal not begotten, self-existent, great and compassionate.
The True was at the beginning, the True was at the distant part.
The True is at the present, O Nanak, the True will be also in the future.'

This is how the book of Genesis pictures God creating the world:

THE SEVEN DAYS OF CREATION

DAY 1

Then God commanded, "Let there be light" – and light appeared. Then he separated the light from the darkness, and he named the light "Day" and the darkness "Night". Evening passed and morning came – that was the first day.'

DAY 2

Then God commanded, "Let there be a dome to divide the water and to keep it in two separate places" – and it was done... He named the dome "Sky". Evening passed and morning came – that was the second day.

DAY 3

Then God commanded, "Let the water below the sky come together in one place, so that the land will appear" – and it was done... Then he commanded, "Let the earth produce all kinds of plants, those that bear grain and those that bear fruit" – and it was done... And God was pleased with what he saw. Evening passed and morning came – that was the third day.

DAY 4

Then God commanded, "Let lights appear in the sky to separate day from night"... and it was done. So God made the two larger lights, the sun to rule over the day and the moon to rule over the night; he also made the stars... And God was pleased with what he saw. Evening passed and morning came – that was the fourth day.

DAY 5

Then God commanded, "Let the water be filled with many kinds of living beings, and let the air be filled with birds." So God created the great sea monsters, all kinds of creatures that live in the water, and all kinds of birds... Evening passed and morning came – that was the fifth day.

DAY 6

Then God commanded, "Let the earth produce all kinds of animal life: domestic and wild, large and small" – and it was done... Then God said, "And now we will make human beings; they will be like us and resemble us. They will have power over the fish, the birds, and all animals..." So God created human beings, making them to be like himself. He created them male and female, blessed them, and said, "Have many children, so that your descendants will live all over the earth and bring it under their control..." God looked at everything he had made and he was very pleased. Evening passed and morning came – that was the sixth day.

DAY 7

And so the whole universe was completed. By the seventh day God finished what he had been doing and stopped working. He blessed the seventh day and set it apart as a special day, because by that day he had completed his creation and stopped working. And that is how the universe was created.

Extracts from Genesis chapters 1 and 2

THE CREATION STORY

Notice certain things about the story in Genesis:
- No proof is given of God – he is not explained.
- The story introduces the absolute beginning of all things. Time and space are both God's creation and so the creation account includes the creation of time itself!
- Genesis does not say whether anything existed before creation.
- God made human beings 'to resemble' himself in some way.
- We are not told what, if anything, he used to create the universe. Early thinkers on the subject said that God created 'out of nothing'. Whereas we have to make a table or a chair or a car out of something which already exists, God's creativity was different – he didn't need anything, it all came from him.
- The creation did not take place all at once, but in different 'phases' or days. It had an order to it.

WHAT PEOPLE BELIEVE ABOUT GENESIS

SOME SAY that the first chapter of the Book of Genesis in the Bible, the account of God creating all the different kinds of creatures in 6 days, was like a scientific account – it happened exactly like that.

SOME SAY each day represents a phase of time in which life developed. So the writer uses the days of the week to illustrate the idea that God created in a certain order and that he completed his work.

SOME SAY God created everything there is using natural processes such as evolution.

SOME SAY they don't believe in the Bible account, but they do believe in a supreme being who created all living things.

SOME SAY that because the form of writing is like that of other ancient tablets, the days of the creation story are the days in which the story was revealed to the writer.

The Mona Lisa by Leonardo da Vinci, the world's most famous painting. The Mona Lisa could be described as a sheet of canvas, a few grams of paint, and the four bits of wood that make up its frame. But there is a lot more to it than that. In the same way, human beings are much more than the collection of chemicals that makes up their bodies.

THE EVOLUTIONARY THEORY

There are various theories of the origin of the universe. One is that there was a time when all the matter in the universe was concentrated into a hot ball. In time this exploded, the matter flew apart and eventually cooled forming first atoms, and then gases and eventually galaxies. This is the **big bang theory**. Some say this happened by chance, others say it was the way God created the world.

During the first half of the nineteenth century, scientists began to study very seriously the form of fossils. Charles Darwin (1809–82) and Alfred Wallace (1823–1913), independently of each other, came to the same explanation of how life developed. They said that a process of *mutation* and *natural selection* was the cause for the amazing variety of life forms from the original living cell. For example, if a wild animal has better hearing or speed than is usual because of a mutation in the cells of the ear or the brain, then it will be a better hunter and therefore healthier than others of its kind. Eventually this sort of animal will replace the other type whose hearing and speed is not so acute.

WHAT PEOPLE BELIEVE ABOUT EVOLUTION

SOME SAY that small molecules (for example ammonia, water) subjected to incredible heat led to the formation of other molecules important to life. Then a series of 'accidents' led to a collection of molecules that could reproduce itself. This was the first living cell. Everything that is alive today has descended from this first cell.

SOME SAY that although they believe in a process of development, they are not convinced that mutation and natural selection could produce the enormous changes needed to change apes into humans or fish into amphibians.

SOME SAY that the evolutionary theory causes us to expect some

OH NO!
I CAN FEEL AN
EVOLUTIONARY
CHANGE
APPROACHING...

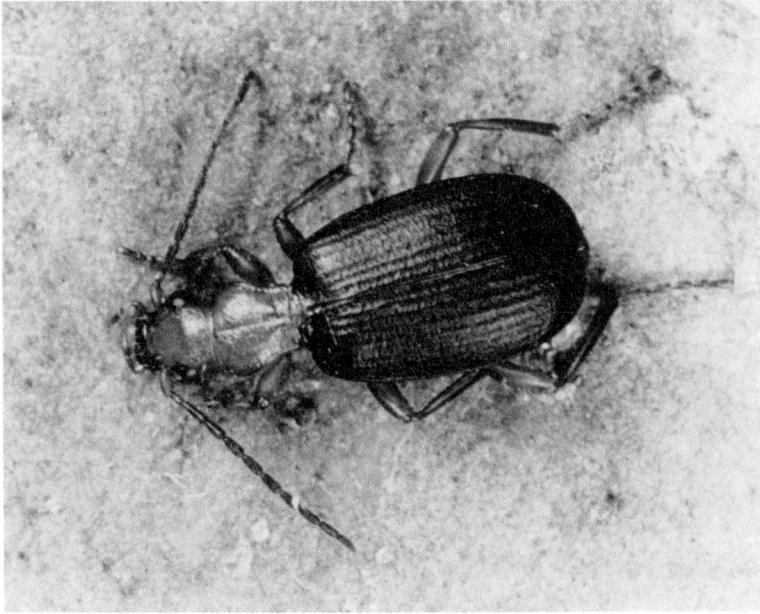

The Bombardier Beetle is a pest for those who believe in evolution. It stores in its body two chemicals which explode when mixed. So to stop itself from being blown to bits, the beetle adds an *inhibitor* to the mixture which prevents the explosion. But when an enemy approaches, it squirts the mixture out, adds an *anti-inhibitor*, and bang! Creationists say that this complicated defence mechanism had to be created all at once – it could not have developed gradually. If you miss out one part, the beetle's ancestors would quickly have died out.

BANG!

WHOOPS!

sort of 'between' creature as one type evolved into another. Yet there are large numbers of 'missing links'.

SOME SAY that not only does the idea of evolution explain the development of natural life, it can also be applied to the development of the human race to ever higher achievements. However this 'evolutionist' theory has taken rather a knock this century because of all the things which have happened to show that people are *not* necessarily so developed after all!

THE CREATION/EVOLUTION CONTROVERSY

As far as humanity is concerned the problem revolves around what is meant by being made 'to resemble' God, or put another way 'made in God's image'. If it is taken to mean qualities God gave to a particular animal somewhere in history, then creationists can accept the scientific view of human development. But if the idea of 'being made in God's image' requires that God made the human body and soul in a separate act, apart from animals, then people who believe in creation must part company with evolutionary theory at this point.

·F·O·L·L·O·W·U·P·

1. Divide a page into seven parts and use each section to illustrate colourfully the seven 'days' of creation. Label each section according to its order (e.g. Day 1, Day 2, etc).

2. Explain what is meant by the following:
○ Evolution   ○ Creation
○ Natural Selection   ○ Fossil
○ Mutation

3. Evaluate what you see as the strengths and weaknesses of either a) a creationist view or b) an evolutionist view. Set your work out in two columns, and try to find three pluses and three problems with the theory you have chosen.

EVOLUTION	
THE CONVINCING POINTS	**THE WEAKNESSES**
1. It explains what we have found in fossils.	**1.** Scientists haven't found fossils to fit in with all the changes needed for this theory.
2. _____	**2.** _____
3. _____	**3.** _____

God on Trial

REV. RICKY

In the last section of this book we glanced quickly at some of the main theories about the formation of life and its development. All of them have their problems and a long time could be spent in discussing each one. The purpose of this chapter is to look at the creation theory and the whole idea of whether there is a God behind the creation of the world. It is easy to come out with a definite 'No way!' or a more positive 'Of course there's a God!' without having thought about it too much. Firstly, let's look at what puts people off the idea of God and religion and then we will look at what gets them interested.

·F·O·L·L·O·W·U·P·

1. If you had absolute control in the world would you force people to be good? Give reasons for your answer.

2. Which of the objections can you identify with? Write a paragraph on what puts you off religious faith.

3. Do you ever pray? Here are some answers, a number of which were given by fifteen-year-olds:
○ I pray when I'm depressed.
○ I've never prayed.
○ I prayed once when I was in trouble – real trouble – and things got better.
○ I prayed when my brother was in a car accident. He recovered, but it didn't mean I believed in God.
○ I pray every day that God will help me.

4. What do you think prayer is? Is it:
○ Asking God's help for yourself?
○ Asking God's help for other people less fortunate than you?
○ Getting to know God better by talking to him?
○ Thinking about God?
○ Thinking about the good things in life?
○ Concentrating on yourself?
Or is it something else? What do you think?

REVEREND RICKY'S RELIGIOUS RIDDLE PAGE

This week the Reverend answers your objections about religion . . .

> **God has never done anything for me. Why should I believe in him?**
>
> *Ethel from Edinburgh*

Some people might disagree with your statement that God has done nothing for you. If he exists then he might have created you! Keep an open mind and ask other people, especially any Christians you bump into, if God has done anything for them. He may be doing a great deal but you don't realize it.

> **I prayed and it didn't work.**
>
> *Dave from Durham*

When I was younger I felt just the same – that prayer didn't work. I used to pray that God would give me the things I wanted. When he didn't appear to do anything, I stopped believing for a while. God must have taken my attempts at prayer very seriously because since then I've understood more what prayer is and instead of giving up on God I've grown to know him more and more. Keep on praying and ask his help to pray properly.

> **The Church is full of hypocrites and old women.**
>
> *Sid from Scunthorpe*

There are hypocrites everywhere – the church is no exception. How often do you know what is right but you don't do it? Yet just as one vandal in a football crowd doesn't mean all supporters are thugs, so in a church there are a lot of sincere people and they're not all old women – at least, not in my church!

> **If there's a God why doesn't he stop all the wars in the world or heal all the sick people?**
>
> *Sharon from Sheerness*

I don't know the whole answer to this question. If I was God I'd probably wipe out all the murderers and terrorists and there would be no sickness. But he doesn't. One thing I have found helpful is to remember that some evil is caused by *people themselves* – the Bible says that mankind has fallen a long way from being 'like God' or 'in his image'. Instead, people have chosen to live life their own way. I wonder how much sickness and poverty could be avoided if enough people decided to share their food and money with others less fortunate.

Some say that if God is all powerful he should *force* us to be good, and stop all the wars etc. However he doesn't use force – perhaps other readers could write in and give us their opinion?

Why Believe in God?

When a person says they believe in God it is always interesting to find out why. There are literally hundreds of reasons people have for believing in God – if they are not too embarrassed to tell you about them.

Two boys did a school project on why people believe in God. In the four groups below are some of the reasons people gave when they were interviewed.

PEOPLE WITH REASONS

GROUP 1

There must be someone or something that started all of us lot off, mustn't there? I mean, even if it all started in a Big Bang we've come a long way since the dinosaurs haven't we? And I just can't believe that cats and dogs and great whales – and me – all happened by accident. I mean, we're all so different aren't we?

If the world and everything in it all happened by chance, then everything today happens by chance too. Every baby, leaf, flower, fish happens by chance, you can't suddenly believe in laws. But I believe there are laws governing our universe, so there must be a law-giver, someone who orders it.

Everything is designed so carefully. Take the human eye, for example – it's a masterpiece of planning. When things are so wonderfully designed there must be someone who designed them, a very intelligent designer.

GROUP 2

PEOPLE WITH EXPERIENCE

Other people believe in God not because of well thought out arguments, but because they have had some sort of experience. A supernatural experience is one that can't quite be explained away by natural means.

Then there are human experiences which take us by surprise. So often we go about our daily lives, eating, working, sleeping and laughing without a thought of how and why we exist. But on rare occasions we are suddenly aware of living and dying and how limited our lives are. Here are some of these sorts of experiences:

● A sudden awareness that I am 'me', distinct from everyone and everything else.
● A realization of how limited life is and a fear of dying.
● The feeling that you have been here before, or done this action before (called deja vu).
● You have prayed for something and it has happened.
● A coincidence you can't explain away or something highly unlikely occurs.
● A feeling of intense joy and happiness for no apparent reason.
● You discover resources of strength and ability to face a very difficult situation.
● An out-of-the-body experience as if I am looking down on myself from above.

GROUP 4

PEOPLE WITH REASONS AND EXPERIENCE OF GOD

A few who were interviewed said that in addition to their reasons they felt they had had an experience of God. This is illustrated by the following two stories . . .

WATCHING THE ANTS

'When I was about five I had the experience on which in a sense my life has been based. It has always remained real and true for me. Sitting in the garden one day I suddenly became conscious of a colony of ants in the grass, running rapidly and purposefully about their business. Pausing to watch them I studied the form of their activity, wondering how much of their own pattern they were able to see for themselves. All at once I knew that I was so large that, to them, I was invisible – except, perhaps, as a shadow over their lives. I was gigantic, huge – able at one glance to comprehend at least to some extent the work of the whole colony. I had the power to destroy or scatter it, and I was completely outside the sphere of their knowledge and understanding. They were part of the body of the earth. But they knew nothing of the earth except the tiny part of it which was their home.

'Turning away from them to my surroundings, I saw that there was a tree not far away, and the sun was shining. There were clouds and blue sky that went on for ever and ever. And suddenly I was tiny – so little and weak and insignificant that it didn't really matter at all whether I existed or not. And yet, insignificant as I was, my mind was capable of understanding that the limitless world I could see was beyond my comprehension. I could know

GROUP **3**

PEOPLE WITH NO REASONS OR DIRECT EXPERIENCE

A percentage of people interviewed believed in God although they had no real reasons or experiences:

I've always believed in him since I was a child, although I never go to church, but I pray every day.

Believing in God is natural to me, I would find it hard not to.

I went to Sunday school as a kid and I was brought up in a Christian family where we all went to church, so of course I believe.

myself to be a minute part of it all. I could understand my lack of understanding . . .

'It was a lovely thing to have happened. All my life, in times of great pain or distress or failure, I have been able to look back and remember, quite sure that the present agony was not the whole picture and that my understanding of it was limited as were the ants in their comprehension of their part in the world I knew.'

A CRY FROM THE HEART

'In my confusion and my despair at losing my only son through cancer, I turned to God, who, the Bible says, lost his only son. Mine was a cry for help. "I know you exist, give me a reason to live again," I cried. Slowly and surely a calm and a peace of mind descended upon me. God himself drew near.'

All these kinds of reasons and experiences can cause people to explore the spiritual dimension of life. They begin to accept that there might be a different order of reality existing alongside our own. None of them 'prove' conclusively that there is a God, but some 70 per cent of all those interviewed in the school project said that they believed in God for reasons like those mentioned here.

·F·O·L·L·O·W·U·P·

1. Which of these reasons or experiences do you find most convincing? Why? If you don't find any of them strong enough as a basis for belief, what sort of things would you find helpful?

2. Write about any unusual experience you have had or heard about, which you can't quite explain.

3. Copy out the unusual experiences listed in this section – can you add to the list?

Picturing God

WHO IS GOD?

Is God a 'he', a 'she' or an 'it'?

Is God separate from the world or is there a bit of God in everything?

Where is God? On another planet?

Does he/she communicate with people?

Can we know him? If so, how?

Is he good? If so, why does he allow war, disease and suffering?

Why has he/she made me? Is he interested in me?

Can he see all that is going on in the world at the same moment of time?

Does he listen to prayer?

Does he have likes and dislikes? What sort of personality does he have?

Does God have a future for us after death?

Does he punish those who do evil and does he reward good?

In the last chapter we read about the many reasons and experiences that lead people to believe that God exists. In the United States, a national Gallup Poll in 1978 revealed that something like 50 million adult Americans believe they have had a religious experience. A survey in December 1979 said that 73 per cent of the British population believed in God. Of course, if we asked those same people what *sort* of God they believed in we would probably get very varied descriptions. Some might say, 'An old man with a long beard who sits in heaven on a throne surrounded by angels.' Others might envisage a pulsating life force that energizes everything that lives.

RELIGIONS – AREN'T THEY ALL THE SAME?

We begin to wonder which of these is true – or perhaps none of them are true. Some people think that choosing your religion is like going into a supermarket and choosing which soap powder you prefer as long as it does the job. On this view, all religions are more or less all the same. They fill a human need. However, all religions are not the same. Even in a greatly simplified chart, like the one here, we can see that each religion has quite distinct things to say.

If you examine the chart carefully you will see there are similarities between the major world faiths. For instance, all of them recognize the struggle of

Is God 'the Great Architect', who designed and set the Universe going?

Is God some kind of impersonal Cosmic Force?

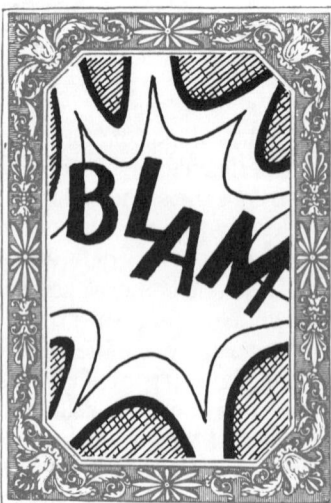

Is God a severe, authority-figure, out to stop us from enjoying ourselves?

good and evil and urge their followers to resist what they believe to be evil and aim for what is good. There is a universal belief in life after death, although Hindus and Buddhists believe in a series of rebirths, while Muslims, Christians and Jews do not. If we were to study further we would find that themes such as pity for the weak, a love of your neighbour and a love of justice are all common ground. But the differences are also great. Here are two examples:

WHAT IS GOD LIKE?

● In Islam, God is beyond human experience. He cannot be found on earth.
● In Hinduism, God is everywhere and is in everything.
● In Buddhism, there is no explicit teaching about God.
● In Christianity, God has shown us what he is like by coming in the human form of Jesus.
● In Judaism, God acts for his people in their history. He can be known because of what he does.

HOW SHOULD WE LIVE?

What you believe influences how you live your life. The differences between the great world religions show this clearly:
● Hindus believe that this life is a consequence of how you lived your last one. Because of this it is easier to accept hardship, poverty and sickness. If your life is hard, it's your own fault. This does not encourage change as improvement belongs to your next life.
● Muslims believe that good and evil both come from Allah. Because of this, improving society does not seem very important to many Muslims. Muslims believe that 'it is the will of Allah' that poverty, sickness and disasters happen. It is the Muslim's duty simply to surrender to his will.
● Christians believe that a lot of social inequality and injustice is a result of people following their own selfish desires rather than obeying God. Because of this, they believe that things in society need to change. It is the Christian's duty to challenge evil and oppression and replace it with good.

PLURALISTIC SOCIETY:
A society where many different religions or beliefs exist alongside each other. No single religion dominates.

Although these illustrations are oversimplified, they illustrate that all religions are *not* more or less the same. The world religions are very different not only in what they believe God is like, but also in the way believers live their lives.

Is God a Grandfather who will smile and shrug his shoulders when we go wrong?

Is God at our beck and call – we expect him to help when we're in trouble?

Is there a God at all?

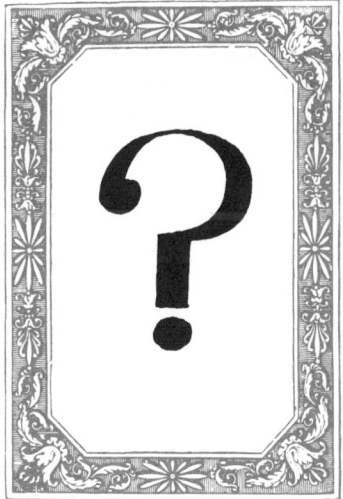

Religion	Date of Founding	Founder	Placcs practised	Holy Books	Life after Death	Belief in God	On Living
Hinduism	1500 BC	None	India	Vedas	Re-incarnation. After this life a person is reborn. Future status depends on present behaviour.	God is a neutral power, a spiritual force that is everything and in everything.	All life is suffering and an illusion. The aim of life is to find release from the continued cycle of rebirth by doing good deeds.
Buddhism	560 BC	Gautama	Far East	Tripitake Sutras	Re-birth similar to Hinduism.	No God originally. Now some worship Buddha.	All life is suffering. Release comes in being able to discipline the mind and "cut off" from the problems of life.
Islam	AD 570	Muhammad	N.W. Africa, Turkey, Syria as far as China	Qu'ran	No re-birth. There is life after death and a day of judgment when people give an account of their actions.	God is Allah. He cannot be known, he is too great. Evil and good come from him.	A Muslim must release himself to the will of Allah. To fulfil Allah's will he keeps the five pillars of Islam: Belief, prayer, fasting, giving money to the poor, pilgrimage.
Judaism	1900 BC 1200 BC	Abraham Moses	All over the world	The Torah	Very little in the Torah about life after death. Nowadays many Jews believe in after-life and the resurrection of the body.	One God, the Lord. His character can be known through what he has done in Israel's history.	The Jews are a people who were released by God from slavery in Egypt (1200 BC). Their response was to live lives that keep God's laws in the Old Testament.
Christianity	4 BC	Jesus of Nazareth (later called Jesus Christ)	All over the world	The Bible	Christians believe in an after-life and in the resurrection of the body. They also believe that God will re-create the whole Universe.	God is creator and Father of Jesus Christ. He can be known because his spirit is at work in the life of a Christian, making God a reality.	A Christian has been released from the slavery of selfishness. Because of Jesus' life, death and resurrection, he or she is given the power to serve God and other people.

F·O·L·L·O·W·U·P

1. Draw the following chart and fill in the spaces with your answers. Try looking at them in a year or so and see if they are the same.

Do you believe in God? If your answer is 'yes' say why and what sort of God you believe in. If your answer is 'no' say why and then explain if you believe in anything else.	Yes, I believe in God because . . .
What do you think happens after this life?	I think that when you die . . .
Do you think that people are good or evil or a mixture of both? Why?	I think that people are . . .

2. We live in a **pluralistic society** where there are many minority groups with different religious beliefs and practices. Take any large town or city and you will be able to trace people from Asia, India, Europe, Africa, the Americas, the Far East. Imagine yourself having to move and settle in a new country. Which of the following would you find most difficult:

● Finding your way around a new place.
● Misunderstanding what people say because you don't know the language very well.
● Being unemployed because of prejudice, or because you haven't got references from people in this new country.
● People being unfriendly and aggressive to you because you're foreign.

● Living your life differently (different clothes, food, behaviour) and being thought stupid because you're different.

These are just a few of the things that are difficult for immigrants to a foreign country. Copy out the list and see if you can add to it.

Idols: Gods of Our Own Making

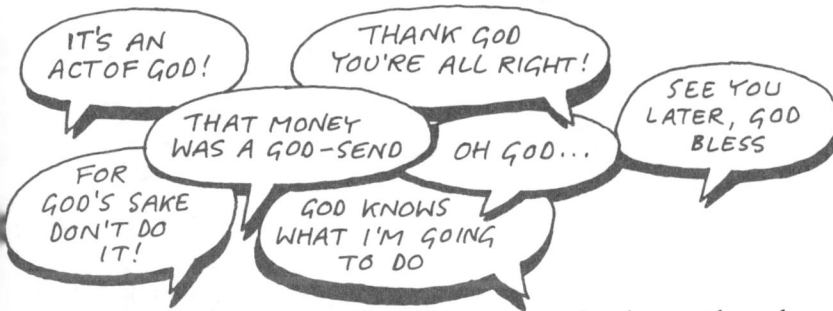

IT'S AN ACT OF GOD!

THANK GOD YOU'RE ALL RIGHT!

SEE YOU LATER, GOD BLESS

THAT MONEY WAS A GOD-SEND

OH GOD...

FOR GOD'S SAKE DON'T DO IT!

GOD KNOWS WHAT I'M GOING TO DO

All of these sayings refer to God. Yet most people who use them do so out of habit rather than for any other reason. But all of them assume a belief, however vague, in some superhuman being who has power over nature and human fortunes. This being is therefore greater than ordinary humans and should be worshipped.

What people worship shows what is most important to them. To worship means much more than liking or loving or respecting someone. To worship is to adore, to devote yourself to, to regard something or someone as God-like. Not everyone worships. Some people can't believe that there is anything worth that sort of devotion. Others worship, but they don't give their adoration to God. Instead they give their undivided loyalty to another person. We call this 'idolizing'. An idol is someone or something that is the object of excessive devotion. It is either man or man-made and it replaces God because it gives meaning to life.

TODAY'S IDOLS

In the Bible, idols were *false* gods, man-made statues that were obeyed and worshipped.

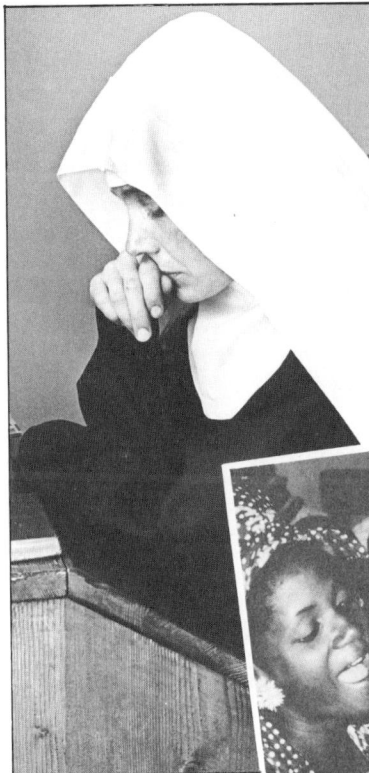

For Christians, worshipping God can be exciting or quiet, as shown by these two pictures. Excited worshippers argue that if people can get excited about football matches or Christmas presents, then God, who is much greater, deserves our excitement, too. Quiet worshippers stress the need to listen to what God is saying to us.

THERE IS THE THIRTEEN YEAR-OLD JULIET WHO 'IDOLIZES' THE FIFTEEN YEAR OLD ROMEO.

THERE IS THE SUPER-EGO MEGASTAR WHO DAZZLES AT THE DISCO AND IDOLIZES HIS OWN BODY.

THERE IS THE FOOTBALL FANATIC WHO NOT ONLY ENJOYS THE GAME BUT LIVES, BREATHES, SLEEP AND WORSHIPS THE TEAM.

To many of us in our society, it would be strange if we returned home each evening to bow before a statue in our bedroom or to offer it food and gifts. But in other parts of today's world it is not so strange. Although we may or may not worship idols, there are other things that we give excessive devotion to and that exert a certain amount of control over us.

There is a difference between someone who enjoys and takes part in football, discos, cars, and so on, and somone who treats them as objects of worship. All of them give a purpose for living but they are not worth our worship. Their only importance is the importance that we, as people, attach to them. In this way they are man-made and could be called idols if worshipped.

TRUE WORSHIP

True worship means that the object of devotion is not human or of human origin but that it exists apart from any importance we attach to it. For this reason, discovering God is difficult because it means our man-made conception of what he is like is not enough. It would be so much easier if we could wrap God up like a present, put him in a box and say, 'That's it! I know exactly what God is like.'

If we tried to do this, then God would cease to be God! He would just be another form of human knowledge that we could write a paper on and pass exams in. God, if he exists, must be much more than a human being. He must be something 'other' than us. Discovering him can't be

THERE IS THE ACE ACADEMIC WHO, FORSAKING ALL OTHERS, WORSHIPS HER MIND.

THERE IS THE MOTOR MANIAC WHOSE REASON FOR LIVING IS ADDING MORE CHROME TO HIS CAR.

THERE IS THE ULTRA-COOL WHOSE ABILITY TO SEE THE STUPIDITY OF EVERYBODY ELSE'S STYLE IS WORTHY OF A FOLLOWING.

predictable or as easy as finding out about other things. Yet there are all sorts of people today who claim to have discovered things about God.

In the Bible, people are often surprised by God. He does things that they weren't expecting. A famous author called C.S. Lewis wrote the story of his life in a book called *Surprised by Joy*. He says that for years he proved that God could not exist, but then to his surprise found God to be a reality. God was still there – whether he believed in him or not.

PEOPLE WHO FOUND GOD

The Bible could be described as a book about people who struggled to know God. For all their problems, they found him to be a real person. Some of these people in the Bible were anything but saintly:

● Moses was a murderer.
● King David committed adultery and then arranged the death of his lover's husband.
● Jael was a tough lady who quietly put a tent peg through a defeated general's skull, while he was asleep.

Yet God was known even by people like these who often became good rebels instead of bad ones and served God powerfully in their day.

·F·O·L·L·O·W·U·P·

INTRODUCING THE 'WHAT I DEVOTE MY TIME TO' CHART

1 Here is a time chart for a week. Copy it out and fill it in according to what you would be doing with your time during a week in your life from 6 a.m. to midnight. Of course not every week is the same, but choose a timetable which reflects a typical week for you.

	MONDAY	TUESDAY	WEDNESDAY	THURSDAY	FRIDAY	SATURDAY	SUNDAY
A.M.							
6							
7							
8							
9							
10							
11							
12							
P.M.							
1							
2							
3							
4							
5							
6							
7							
8							
9							
10							
11							
12							

● What do you give your time and devotion to?
● How many hours do you spend eating? Working? At school? In front of a television? Listening to music? Seeing your friends?
● Design a graph entitled 'Time to Spend'. Count the hours you spend on each activity and colour them in on the graph. Do not include hours you sleep. Now look at what you spend most time on. The results may surprise you!

2 Make your own list of modern 'idols' – things of human origin which people devote themselves to.

Bible Facts

BIBLE I
(THE OLD TESTAMENT)

- All 39 books from Genesis to Malachi
- Including the famous Ten Commandments
- Murder, mystery, suspense

COMING SOON — BIBLE II

BIBLE II
(THE NEW TESTAMENT)

- All 27 books from Matthew to Revelation
- Parables, miracles, the Sermon on the Mount and much more...
- Shipwrecks, snakebites, close encounters

BY THE AUTHOR OF BIBLE I

DID YOU KNOW?

● **THE BIBLE IS A LIBRARY** The word 'Bible' comes from the Greek word *biblia* meaning 'books'. It is made up of sixty-six smaller books, and took many different people more than 1,000 years to write.

● **IT IS DIVIDED INTO TWO IMPORTANT PARTS** The Old Testament (the first half of the Bible) has thirty-nine books, while the New Testament contains twenty-seven books.

● **THE OLD TESTAMENT** was mostly written in the Hebrew language. It was written in Palestine, Babylonia and neighbouring areas. It is the story of a group of nomads who later became the nation of Israel. The Old Testament covers some 2,000 years of their history. They discovered God as the one who was involved and concerned about their lives, and who wanted them to love and obey him. However, the Old Testament repeatedly records the failure of the Israelites to love and obey God.

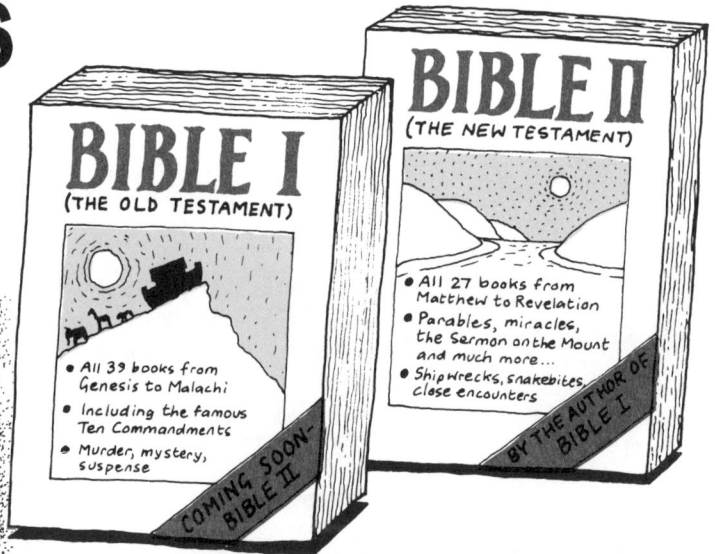

● **THE NEW TESTAMENT** was written in Greek and most of the books date between AD 50 and AD 100.

It begins with the four Gospels. These are accounts of the life, teaching and death of Jesus of Nazareth, an Israelite who claimed in a special way to be God's Son in human form.

Next is the Acts of the Apostles. This is the story of what happened after Jesus' followers discovered that he had been raised from the dead and how they spread this good news around the world.

Thirdly, there are letters written by famous Christians (especially St Paul) to groups of Christian beginners. The letters told them how to live as Christians and how to overcome the many problems and dangers they faced.

Finally, the Book of Revelation is a collection of visions and pictures given to John by God.

● **THE BOOKS OF THE OLD AND NEW TESTAMENT** are not printed in the order in which they were written. It is no good trying to follow through their history from beginning to end simply by reading each book in turn.

● **THE BIBLE CONTAINS LOTS OF DIFFERENT STYLES OF WRITING.** It is not just history! It also contains poetry, codes of law, songs, prophecy, wise sayings, and much more . . .

● **THE BIBLE HAS BEEN TRANSLATED INTO SOME 800 LANGUAGES.** But there is still a long way to go! There are 5,000 known languages in the world, and even then 2,000 of them have not been written down in grammatical form. But it is still true to say that the Bible has been translated more than any other book.

THE·OLD·TESTAMENT

GENESIS

JOSHUA

HISTORY & LAW

HISTORY

JOB

ISAIAH

DRAMA, POETRY PROVERBS

PROPHECY

WHAT THE BIBLE ISN'T

● **THE BIBLE ISN'T JUST A HISTORY OF ISRAEL,** with facts about kings and leaders. If this were so, then a lot has been left out and a lot of unnecessary materials left in.

● **THE BIBLE ISN'T JUST A GREAT PIECE OF LITERATURE.** Although it does have its great moments in powerful stories and moving poetry and songs, the Bible also deals with the mundane facts of everyday life, too. One writer spends twelve verses talking about what to do if you've got mildew. Hardly a piece of literary genius, although if you've got mildew, a best-seller!

● **THE BIBLE ISN'T A SCIENTIFIC TEXT BOOK.** The first chapters of the book of Genesis are not trying to lay down facts about *how* the world was created. Instead, they tell us about *who* created it and *why* it was spoiled. This shows the difference between the Bible's approach and a scientific approach. While science is concerned with accurate descriptions of how things happen, the Bible asks the 'why' questions of human life.

SCIENCE
How did the earth begin?
How is sickness cured?
How does mankind live?
How do people die?

THE BIBLE
Why did earth begin?
Why is there suffering?
Why has mankind gone wrong?
Why do people die and what happens after death?

THE·NEW·TESTAMENT

MATTHEW

ROMANS

BIOGRAPHY HISTORY

LETTERS

2 THESSALONIANS

REVELATION

LETTERS CONTINUED

PROPHECY LETTERS

·F·O·L·L·O·W·U·P·

1. Copy the diagram of the Bible as a library of books. Include the names of all sixty-six books and divide them between the Old and New Testaments.

2. Write your own paragraph entitled 'Facts about the Bible'. Use the information in this book and any other you can find in the library.

A Book Worth Dying For?

OPINION 1

'The Bible is a load of rubbish'
Eric 1984

TUESDAY. THE 3 P.M. R.E. LESSON.

CRASH!

NICE OF YOU TO SHOW UP, ERIC

NOW, LETS GET ON WITH LOOKING AT THE BIBLE

YOU'RE NOT TEACHING **ME** THAT LOAD OF RUBBISH! THE BIBLE IS FOR MORONS

THAT'S RIGHT!

TELL HER, ERIC

WHAT DO YOU MEAN? HAVE YOU EVER READ IT?

NAAAA!

ERIC, WHAT IF I HADN'T EVER MET YOU AND I SAID THAT YOU AND YOUR GANG AND YOUR MUSIC WERE A LOAD OF RUBBISH? WHAT WOULD YOU THINK OF ME?

I'D THINK **YOU** WERE A LOAD OF RUBBISH

WELL, THAT'S WHAT I THINK OF YOUR OPINIONS! YOU COME IN HERE AND SAY THAT MY SUBJECT AND THE BIBLE ARE A LOAD OF RUBBISH WHEN YOU DON'T KNOW THE FIRST THING ABOUT IT.

IT'S A GOOD JOB THAT GOD DOESN'T THINK YOU'RE A LOAD OF RUBBISH!

TO HER SURPRISE, ERIC COULDN'T THINK OF AN ANSWER AND THE CLASS WENT SILENT. ERIC KEPT QUIET FOR THE REST OF THE LESSON.

If we were to continue the story of Eric (which is a true-life situation) then we would have to say that Eric, although disruptive and rude, was also honest when faced with a challenge. He went on to give the Bible a fair hearing and made his own decision based on personal enquiry rather than the prejudices of other people.

OPINION 2

'I wish that the Scriptures (the Bible) might be translated into all languages, so that not only the Scots and Irish, but also the Turk and the Saracen might read and understand them. I long that the farm-labourer might sing them as he follows the plough, the weaver hum them to the tune of his shuttle, the traveller beguile the weariness of his journey with their stories.'
Erasmus c1516 AD

To Eric the Bible was trash, to Erasmus it was treasure. Eric would like to put the Bible on the nearest rubbish tip. Erasmus, a famous Dutch scholar, would love everyone to know and learn it.

Through the ages there have been countless people who thought there was something special about the Bible. To them it was more than a history book or a great piece of literature – somehow God spoke through it to men and women. It was a book that changed lives. Some people have even risked their lives to try to make the Bible available for others. Do you know of a book that you would risk your life for? John Wycliffe took risks and William Tyndale actually died to make the Bible available to ordinary people.

JOHN WYCLIFFE
Wycliffe was the first to attempt to translate the whole Bible into English. Although others had made translations of parts of the Bible into Saxon and Old English, their purpose had been simply to serve the clergy. Wycliffe's purpose was to bring the Bible to the ordinary people.

He began to translate the Bible in 1378, working from Latin into English. There was no printing in those days and so his friends copied scores and scores of Wycliffe's Bibles by hand. Take a look at the size of a Bible and you can imagine what hard work it would be just to reproduce one copy. In fact it took about ten months to write one copy of the New Testament. Although the Bibles were burned, people still managed to get copies.

WILLIAM TYNDALE
William Tyndale, in 1522, wanted to translate the Greek New Testament into English, but the Bishop of London refused him permission. Tyndale decided that it was better to obey God and make the Bible available for people than to obey a corrupt church. He had copies of the New Testament printed abroad on the newly-invented printing presses and smuggled them into England. Large numbers arrived and were distributed, but Tyndale was arrested. On 6 October 1536 he was strangled at the stake and burned to ashes.

THE MODERN TRANSLATORS
There are still people today who take large risks and dedicate their lives to making the Bible available to the world. They do this because they believe that if the Bible is read with an open mind, it can help people to know God.

Erasmus, the 16th century scholar. Until his time, all books had to be written out by hand. But the invention of printing allowed Erasmus's books to spread widely and influenced many people.

John Wycliffe. He made many enemies by translating the Bible into ordinary English. He was thrown out of Oxford University and threatened with death – but nothing would stop him.

An illuminated letter 'h' from the Book of Kells.

William Tyndale's execution. His last recorded words appear in the speech bubble. He prayed that the King of England would allow Bibles to be printed in English.

Monks, who copied out the Bible by hand before printing was invented, used to fill the pages with intricate illustrations. Such manuscripts were called 'illuminated' manuscripts. These three dogs are from the Book of Kells, Ireland. In the original, the circle is 5/16 inch in diameter.

·F·O·L·L·O·W·U·P·

1. Wycliffe and Tyndale suffered for what they believed in. Is there anything you feel so strongly about which you would be prepared to take risks for?

2. Look at the illuminated lettering which is shown in this section. Make up your own prayer and spend time 'illuminating' the first letter (which should be bigger than the rest). This is what the monks used to do when they copied Bible manuscripts.

WYCLIFFE'S TRANSLATION 1384

God that spak sum tyme bi prophetis in many manneres to oure fadris, at the last in these daies he hath spoke to us bi the sone; whom he hath ordeyned eir of alle thingis, and bi whom he made the worldis. Which whanne also he is the brightnesse of glorie, and figure of his substance and berith alle thingis bi word of his vertu, he makith purgacioun of synnes, and syttith on the righthalf of the maieste in heuenes; and so mych is maad betere than aungels, bi hou myche he hath eneritid a more dyuerse name bifor hem.

AUTHORIZED VERSION, 1611

God, who at sundry times and in divers manners spake in time past unto the fathers by the prophets, hath in these last days spoken unto us by his Son, whom he hath appointed heir of all things, by whom also he made the worlds; who being the brightness of his glory, and the express image of his person, and upholding all things by the word of his power, when he had by himself purged our sins, sat down on the right hand of the Majesty on high; being made so much better than the angels, as he hath by inheritance obtained a more excellent name than they.

GOOD NEWS BIBLE, 1976

In the past God spoke to our ancestors many times and in many ways through the prophets, but in these last days he has spoken to us through his Son. He is the one through whom God has created the universe, the one whom God has chosen to possess all things at the end. He reflects the brightness of God's glory and is the exact likeness of God's own being, sustaining the universe with his powerful word. After achieving forgiveness for the sins of mankind, he sat down in heaven at the right-hand side of God, the Supreme Power. The Son was made greater than the angels just as the name God gave him is greater than theirs.

BOOK 1

Part Two
COVENANT

The first section of this book looked at some of the big questions in life and whether people think God exists or not. In the second half of the book we look at accounts of people who not only say God exists but who claim to have some sort of relationship or agreement with God. This is called a 'covenant'.

   This section begins by looking at how we make or break our own relationships and agreements with other people (for example, friendships and marriage). It then takes a look at how people have made and broken relationships and agreements with God.

Making Friends, Breaking Friends

If you were asked to write down in one sentence what you think a friend is, what would you say? It would be difficult to choose just one thing because friendship includes very different ingredients. Which of the following definitions do you rate highly?

A FRIEND. . .

- is someone you see and talk to regularly
- is someone you can trust with your secrets
- won't talk about you behind your back
- sticks up for you when you're in trouble
- is someone you like to be with
- has many of the same interests and aims
- is someone you respect and look up to
- is interested in what you have to say
- wants you to succeed and be happy
- doesn't always want his or her own way
- is someone who says sorry when they've hurt you
- always tries to do what is best for you even when he or she risks your disagreement
- is someone who knows your faults – and still likes you

All of these definitions express different ideas about what a friend is. For some people, a friend is anyone they see regularly and know something about. For others, friendship goes a lot further and requires a large degree of trust and loyalty.

A relationship is rather like a building. It has a foundation, then it has the basic materials which form the structure and then the bricks and cement. It takes time and effort to build and some parts are easier to put together than others. It is useful to recognize what makes a good building and what makes a bad, shaky one.

HOW TO BUILD RELATIONSHIPS

● **FOUNDATION** If you set out to build a house, you will need to lay a foundation before anything else. You will have to use a lot of hard muscle by digging below the surface of the ground and making a firm base able to hold the weight and structure of the house. If the foundation is shaky, the whole building is shaky.

This is also true in starting a relationship. Both parties must like each other and want to develop the friendship. If not, it will be very one-sided and one of the people will get hurt and disappointed. Along with the desire for a particular friendship is a sense of need. It's no good saying, 'I'm alright on my own, thank you,' because we all need friends and people to share our lives with.

● **STRUCTURE** The structure gives the general shape to the house, and decides whether it will be a small town house or a skyscraper.

In a relationship, the structure

grows by sharing time and interests. A friendship cannot grow without time spent together. This is what makes it either superficial or valuable. If you only spend one hour of one Saturday every month together then you can't expect to be on close terms with each other. Other things which give structure to a relationship are *interests* (sport, music, fashion, hobbies) and also sharing – and listening to – each other's problems. Good friends also share their successes and achievements – without getting jealous!

● **CEMENT** The cement is the 'glue' that holds the whole thing together. Without cement, a house would very quickly collapse.

The cement of a good relationship is love and forgiveness. You may find that you spend time and share interests with a friend, and yet the friendship doesn't seem able to take the ups and downs of life. For example, you might have an argument and it's weeks before either of you are talking again. This is because the cement of a good relationship is too thin. There is not enough patience or forgiveness. In a word, there is not enough love.

> Good relationships depend on people not holding grudges.
> Good relationships depend on give and take.
> Good relationships do not mean you always give in but nor do they mean that you insist that you are always right.

HOW TO DEMOLISH RELATIONSHIPS

Introducing

The Society for the Extermination of Love and Friendship

We, the above society, SELF for short, pledge ourselves to the following, namely:

The **Promotion** of **Rights** for **Individual Development** to the **Exclusion** of others.

Hereinafter called PRIDE.

This is our aim and sacred charge that at all times our members must commit themselves at home, work and school to PRIDE:

P for Promotion — I promise that I will at all times and in all places look after number one first, that is, me.

R for Rights — I will insist that I am in the right even if I suspect I am in the wrong or partly to blame.

I for Individual — I will strengthen my individuality and protect my right to be me. I will, therefore, never be the first to say sorry as this is a sign of weakness.

D for Development — I will develop my own sensitivity to other people's needs as a service to mankind provided it does not interfere with my time, money or plans.

E for Exclusion — In the event of a loss of self-confidence I will exclude and put others down by gossip, slander, lies or ridicule so that I can always be on top.

SELF

DEAR AUNTIE...

Dear Agony Aunt,
Help me please,
I'm desperate! I'm in
love with someone, but
he loves my best friend

It all happened a few months ago at the Youth Club. Fiona and I saw him at the same time

But I had to go and serve the coffee. Fiona and Tom got on like a house on fire. And guess who walked who home?

Over the next few months, Tom and Fiona were inseparable

But last Thursday, they had a big row

And today Tom came around to see me

...SO I DON'T KNOW WHETHER TO CARRY ON GOING OUT WITH HER

THIS IS MY BIG CHANCE TO GET TOM! WE'RE MADE FOR EACH OTHER AND I REALLY FANCY HIM!

FIONA'S MY BEST FRIEND. SHE'S ALWAYS TRUSTED ME. I OUGHT TO GET THEM BACK TOGETHER

What should I do?

LEVELS OF FRIENDSHIP

CASUAL ACQUAINTANCE The person you happen to meet from time to time at school, at work or at the youth club.

ACQUAINTANCE This is the person who is included on a regular basis among the people you meet or work with.

ONE OF A NUMBER OF FRIENDS More than an acquaintance, but less than a real friend. This relationship includes the sort of people you have regular conversations with in a group.

A FRIEND Someone you like being with and with whom you share your opinions, your likes and dislikes etc.

A PARTICULAR FRIEND More than a friend, this is one whom you like to spend far more time with, someone you can turn to in trouble and whose opinion you consider important.

A BEST FRIEND Usually a friendship which has taken time to develop and which has been tested. A best friend has a special place and priority in your life. They can depend on you to be loyal and there is usually a strong bond of affection between you.

In a group, you may have many acquaintances, a few friends, and one or two really close friends. The more you have in common with someone, the more likely you are to be friends rather than just acquaintances.

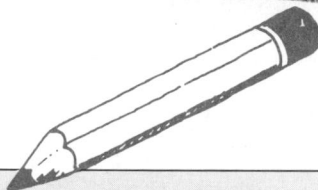

RATE YOURSELF

Look through the three situations below and test your friendship. Pick out your first reaction and check your score.
1. You lend your favourite LP to your friend, who leaves it on the bus. How do you react?
a) Say it's okay but feel angry about it inside.
b) Forgive – after all, that's what friendship is about.
c) Plan revenge.
2. You overhear two people gossiping about your friend. Do you ...
a) Interrupt them and stick up for your friend.
b) Decide to check out the 'facts' with the rest of your mates.
c) Keep an eye on your friend to see if it's true.

3. Your friend's romance has come to an abrupt end. You always fancied him/her yourself. How do you react?
a) Go out with your friend's ex yourself.
b) Say 'At last! It was a complete waste of time.'
c) Take your friend out to see a movie.

How does your friendship rate? Give yourself the following scores for your answers:
1. a2, b3, c1
2. a3, b1, c2
3. a1, b2, c3
Add up your answers.
Only 3 With a friend like you, who needs enemies?
3–7 You're a bit of a fair-weather friend, being loyal only when it suits you. Can your friends really rely on you?
8–9 You're a true friend, loyal, forgiving and generous.
10–12 You may be a great friend, but you need help with maths!

·F·O·L·L·O·W·U·P·

1. Look at the comic strip. Discuss what the girl in the story should do.
2. Write down three characteristics that you look for in a friend, for example, understanding, or a sense of humour. Why are these so important to you?
3. What three things do you most dislike in other people, and why?
4. Write a short account on one of the following:
● The person I admire most.
● My best friend.
5. Look at the box entitled 'A friend ....' Go down the list and instead of reading 'A friend is...' replace it with 'I am ...' beginning at number two: 'I am someone you can trust with your secrets'. If you're honest, this may help you to see ways in which you can improve your friendships.

Good Communication

Have you ever thought how difficult it is to get someone to understand what you're saying? For instance, you might say to a friend something quite innocent like 'I don't want to go to see the film'. The next thing you know they're saying, 'Well, if you want to be like that, I won't go out with you on Saturday'. You might have been trying to say that you weren't in the mood, or you didn't have the money to go to see the film, but that's not what **came across** to your friend.

What we mean to say and what our hearers actually pick up can sometimes be two completely different things. Many people fall out or become enemies simply because of bad communication. Communication may sound a simple thing, but in fact it is quite complicated. Look at 'The Communication Process' box on page 44. It contains a technical breakdown of what is happening when one person sends a message to another.

MORE THAN WORDS

Words are not the only means of communication. Our gestures, facial expressions and body movements are an important part of how we communicate. Some people have even argued that these non-verbal messages are much stronger than our spoken words.

Here are some ways in which we communicate an unintentional message which can sometimes prevent good communication and therefore be a hindrance to making friendships:

● **THE WAY WE SAY SOMETHING** There are a hundred ways of saying 'good morning'. A lot depends on your tone of voice, and not just on the words. If you say it quickly and abruptly, instead of expressing a welcome it communicates a cold, formal greeting that actually says: 'Keep away from me, I don't like you'. This is not always intentional. Sometimes a person intends to give out warmth in his or her voice and fails to do so. It may be nervousness which tightens the muscles and prevents free expression.

● **WHAT WE DO WHEN WE ARE SPEAKING** It is difficult to believe that a person is genuinely interested in you and what you have to say if he or she continually looks around or fidgets when you are having a conversation.

● **OUR FACIAL EXPRESSIONS AND GESTURES** We don't always see ourselves as others do. Perhaps you've seen a photo of yourself, or some film, and you've said 'Do I really look like that?' Your face didn't look as you imagined it to be. Some people have a natural expression of cheerfulness and it can get them into trouble because teachers think they are being silly. Or it can be the opposite. You appear to be stuck-up and snobbish because your facial expression is serious.

● **WHAT YOU WEAR** What a person wears says a lot about them. Appearance is a form of communication. We all sum each other up by the way we speak and dress.

'Body language' is the way that we communicate our feelings without speaking – through facial expressions, movements, and the way that we sit or stand. Notice the way that these two people show their interest in each other by the way they sit, and the distance between them.

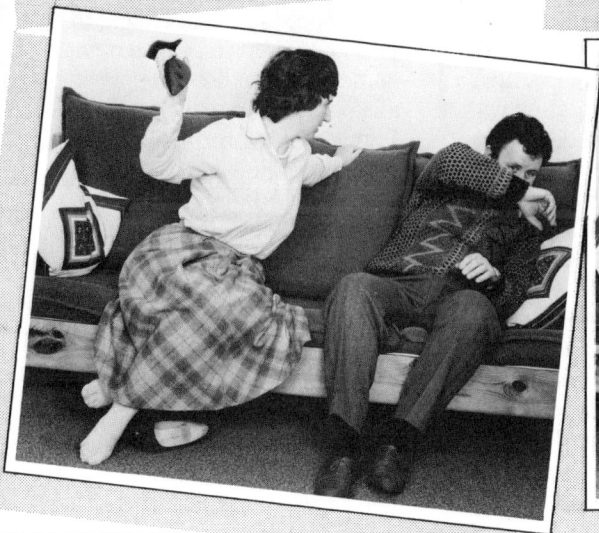

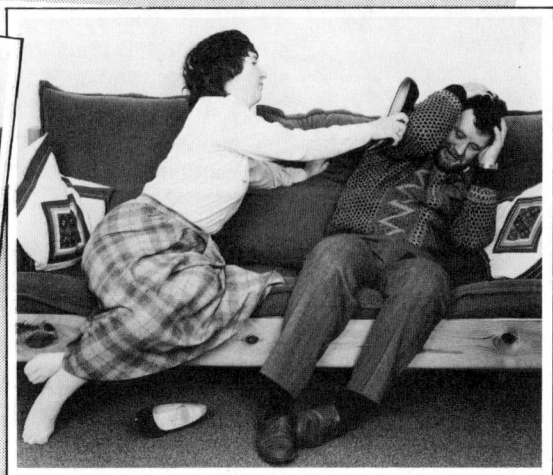

Covering up your mouth can be a way of hiding your true thoughts or feelings from the person talking to you. It's hard to know what this person is thinking.

Eyes tell us a lot about what someone is thinking. Cover them up, and communication gets difficult.

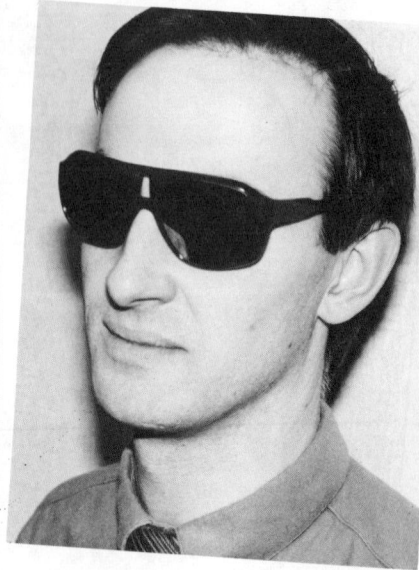

·F·O·L·L·O·W·U·P·

1. Say these two sentences out loud as if you were interested, enquiring, annoyed and worried. You should notice that your tone, pitch and volume varies for each feeling.
○ When are you going?
○ What is this thing called love?

2. Gestures can be used deliberately to replace words. They can often be developed into their own sign language.
Draw your own made up gestures or hand signals which could mean:
○ I don't know
○ I refuse
○ I agree

3. How do we position ourselves?
The way in which we position ourselves in relation to another person (e.g. how far apart, leaning towards or away from) indicates much about our feelings for another person and the situation.
Stand about eight metres apart from a classmate and then slowly approach your friend in short slow steps. When you or your partner feel close enough, ask the other to stop. Then measure the distance between you. This is what has been called your 'personal space'. Some people need more personal space than others, which is why they feel uncomfortable when others get too near. How did your 'space' compare with others in the group?

Someone who turns up for an interview for his first job as a trainee banker in scruffy old jeans and a jumper in holes probably won't get the job. His clothes say that he doesn't want to conform, and that he doesn't care what people think about him. These may or may not be admirable qualities but to be a banker you need to get on with all sorts of people and to make people confident in you. The employer looks at his clothes and therefore thinks he is not suited to the job.

OVER-CONFIDENT OR SHY?
Another thing that can get in the way of communication is our opinion of what we ourselves are like. If we have too high an opinion of ourselves our attitude can be boastful. If we have too

low an opinion then whenever we start a conversation with unknown people we can secretly think: 'I wonder what they think of me?' We become too self-conscious, instead of being natural and free to concentrate on the person we're talking to. It is also *very* difficult if you meet someone with the same problem as yourself!

It is clear from all this that communication is much more than words. It involves all our senses whether we realize it or not, and misunderstanding can happen at every step of the way. It is therefore worth it to be patient, and to try not to be offended easily. Often people don't mean what you think they do. It is also possible to improve your communication skills so that you're not misunderstood.

A Broken Relationship

So far we have looked at friendships between people. Throughout its pages the Bible speaks of friendship between God and people. Sometimes the friendship was very close and sometimes the people doubted and rebelled and the relationship needed re-making.

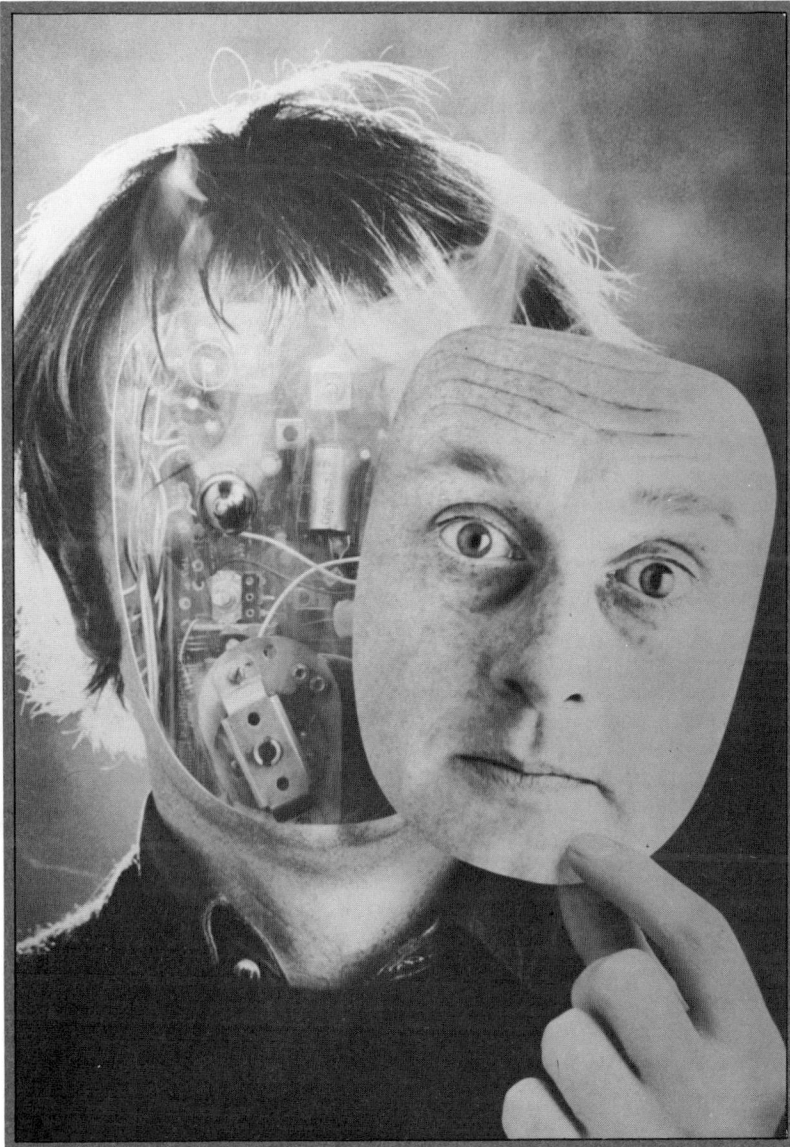

Christians believe that God gave humans the freedom to choose right or wrong. We are not robots, programmed to obey God. Sadly, people chose to disobey. This has led to a great deal of the suffering and misery in our world.

IS IT POSSIBLE?

The re-make is called covenant. The word can mean 'friendship', or it can mean 'agreement' or 'promise'. God makes covenants with people to renew the relationship which has been broken. But all this isn't just ancient history! There are people today, and not just in the Bible, who say that they know God. This raises all sorts of questions. How can you 'know' someone that you can't see? If God wants me to believe then why doesn't he prove himself and appear to me! If you have a relationship with God that must mean conversation – so does God speak? Why don't I hear him if he does?

There are many answers that can be given to these questions, but here are just two possibilities.

- If God exists and I don't experience him then either it's because he's so great and so different to me that communication is impossible, *or* ...
- He does speak and communicate with the human race, but I'm not picking up the message.

POOR COMMUNICATION

Let's refer to our diagram of the communication process. At least three things could be going wrong.

- Perhaps the method God uses for transmission is unknown to me. It might not be speaking or acting, it could be non-verbal communication of which I am not yet aware.
- Perhaps the communication centre is so different between God and me that understanding is difficult. God's values and actions might be so alien to mine that there's little common ground.
- There could be interference which stops the message getting through.

Men and women have always found it difficult to get to know God. Many religions have different stories of a perfect age in our past where God and mankind lived together in harmony. There is widespread acknowledgement that in some way we have fallen a long way from God. The communication has stopped. The Bible explains it with the story of Adam and Eve in the Book of Genesis, chapter three.

THE COMMUNICATION PROCESS

Sender
Person sending the message

Encoding Process
When you transform thoughts and ideas into words or gestures or facial expressions

Transmission
The channel of communication: speech, acting, etc.

Message
What you want to say

Unintentional message
Not words but rather actions or appearance (nodding head, careless dress, habits). All these can alter the verbal message which has been said

Communication Centre
This is the shared experience of both the sender and the receiver of the message, (personality, language social background, values)

Interference
External and internal. External: noise of all sorts, distraction visually.

Internal: pain, tiredness

Reception
The way we receive a message: bodily response, eyes, nose, ears, skin, etc.

Decoding
Transforming words and gestures given from the sender into thoughts

Receiver
The person for whom the message is intended. The receiver needs to acknowledge that the message has arrived and therefore gives 'feedback'

Feedback
If feedback is negative, it means that there is no response or a lack of it. For example:

Sender: 'What do you want to eat?'
Receiver: 'I eat at lunch time.'
The message has not been understood. Feedback can be neutral such as a blank expression on someone's face. Then the message probably needs repeating.

ADAM AND EVE GET IT WRONG

Was there a real Adam and Eve? Some Christians think they were historical people – as real as Elvis Presley or Henry VIII, and that there was a place called the Garden of Eden and a time when animals talked. Many Christians see this more as an inspired story which explains why our relationship with God was spoiled. Whichever way you look at it, the story tells us a lot . . .

BLAH BLAH BLAH BLAH BLAH BLAH BLAH BLAH BLAH BLAH BLAH BLAH BLAH BLAH B...

DOO BE DOO

GOVERNMENT HEALTH WARNING: PERSONAL STEREOS CAN LOSE YOU FRIENDS...

● ABOUT GOD

God wasn't a dictator forcing the people to obey him, neither did he 'programme' them like an android to do what he said. Instead, he gave them the privilege of choice so that they could choose to obey him or not. If obedience was all God wanted he could have easily got it by making a couple of robots, but it seems he wanted a living friendship. You can't force love.

● ABOUT TEMPTATION

Eve was tempted to eat what God had said she shouldn't. It wasn't because she was hungry, rather she was tempted to become like God. So far she had obeyed him and so knew only what good was. But she thought that if she disobeyed him, then she would become wise by knowing about evil. Both Adam and Eve preferred self-rule rather than God's rule. The Bible calls self-rule 'sin'. It is interesting to note that in this story temptation promises us a better deal.

● ABOUT ADAM AND EVE

Before they chose to disobey God, they talked with him and were not ashamed of their nakedness. After they disobeyed, they were ashamed and hid from God. Both of them tried to put the blame elsewhere: Adam blamed Eve, Eve blamed the snake.

● ABOUT THE SIDE EFFECTS OF SELF-RULE

God had warned them that in the day they chose to disobey they would die. Right away, their relationship with God died. In time, they died physically too. The image or likeness of God in them was spoiled, they were excluded from the garden and cut off from God's close friendship.

SOMETHING MISSING

The word 'Adam' means 'mankind' in Hebrew, and although this story is an ancient one it represents a modern problem that is experienced the world over. Many of us feel cut off or excluded as if something

GENESIS CHAPTER 3
ADAM AND EVE DISOBEY GOD

Now the snake was the most cunning animal that the Lord God had made. The snake asked the woman, 'Did God really tell you not to eat fruit from any tree in the garden?'

'We may eat the fruit of any tree in the garden,' the woman answered, 'except the tree in the middle of it. God told us not to eat the fruit of that tree or even touch it; if we do, we will die.'

The snake replied, 'That's not true; you will not die. God said that, because he knows that when you eat it you will be like God and know what is good and what is bad.'

The woman saw how beautiful the tree was and how good its fruit would be to eat, and she thought how wonderful it would be to become wise. So she took some of the fruit and ate it. Then she gave some to her husband and he also ate it. As soon as they had eaten it, they were given understanding and realized that they were naked; so they sewed fig leaves together and covered themselves.

That evening they heard the Lord God walking in the garden, and they hid from him among the trees. But the Lord God called out to the man, 'Where are you?'

He answered, 'I heard you in the garden; I was afraid and hid from you because I was naked.'

'Who told you that you were naked?' God asked. 'Did you eat the fruit that I told you not to eat?'

The man answered, 'The woman you put here with me gave me the fruit, and I ate it.'

The Lord God asked the woman, 'Why did you do this?'

She replied, 'The snake tricked me into eating it . . .'

Then the Lord God said, 'Now the man has become like one of us and has knowledge of what is good and what is bad. He must not be allowed to eat fruit from the tree of life and live for ever.' So the Lord God sent him out of the Garden of Eden and made him cultivate the soil from which he had been formed.

Panel 1: I HATE JENNA, SHE'S SUCH A SHOW-OFF, YET EVERYBODY LIKES HER. I'M TEMPTED TO TELL EVERYONE WHAT SHE'S REALLY LIKE—SHOULD I?

Panel 2: ALL MY FRIENDS HAVE A DECENT STEREO EXCEPT *ME!* I'M TEMPTED TO GET THE MONEY FROM THE SCHOOL OFFICE—THEY'VE GOT PLENTY OF IT! SHOULD I?

Panel 3: I DON'T CARE IF HE *IS* GOING OUT WITH HER! I WANT HIM AND I'M TEMPTED TO GET HIM. SHOULD I?

F·O·L·L·O·W·U·P

1. When the Bible talks about self-rule it uses the word 'sin'. Which of these sins do you think is the worst? Why did you choose this instead of the others?

○ **Stealing** I want to have it.
○ **Gossip** I want to ruin his or her popularity so that I can be number one.
○ **Lying** I want to impress people or I want to get out of trouble.
○ **Bullying** I want them to know I'm boss.
○ **Blaming** I'm too good to be blamed for this.
○ **Showing-off** I have this therefore I'm superior. You don't therefore you're inferior.

2. Temptation is not the same as doing wrong. There is a big difference between wanting to kill someone and actually doing it (especially if you're the victim!). But wanting can lead to doing. Look at the three cartoon pictures. Give your reasons for saying 'yes' or 'no' to the questions.

3. Read through the story in Genesis Chapter 3 and answer the following questions:
○ What was the woman tempted to do?
○ What had God said to the man and the woman?
○ When the woman saw the tree what thoughts did she have about it?
○ Who was the man tempted by?
○ What happened as soon as they had eaten the fruit?
○ What were the consequences of their disobedience?

vitally important is missing from our lives. When people say, 'There must be more to life than this' or 'What's the purpose in it all?' they are expressing a sense of incompleteness and meaninglessness. Such feelings can be put down to unemployment or social problems, but even for people who have everything the problem is not necessarily solved. Every year or so we hear of somebody who appeared to have everything yet who committed suicide out of depression.

Christians call this story in the Book of Genesis 'the fall' because it illustrates how we fell from our high position as God's friends, choosing to go against him and do our own thing.

Introducing Abraham: 'God's Friend'

If you insist on your own way and your friend gets offended then there is a rift between you. It's not until one of you decides to do something or to say sorry that the relationship starts again. Most of us find it hard to say sorry, but if we think we're in the right then we expect the other person to do the apologizing. In the story of Abraham, God takes the initiative to make friends, although he is not to blame for what has happened. We begin by looking at what life was like in the days of Abraham.

DIGGING INTO THE PAST

If you dug down a few feet in your garden you would probably find more than a few worms. There would be remnants of bottles, bits of pottery and so on – in fact, reminders of the last occupants. Archaeology is concerned with the remains of ancient civilizations. An archaeologist *excavates* to find this evidence.

Archaeology can tell us a lot about what life was like for some of the characters we meet in the Bible. The deeper you dig the older the century which you discover.

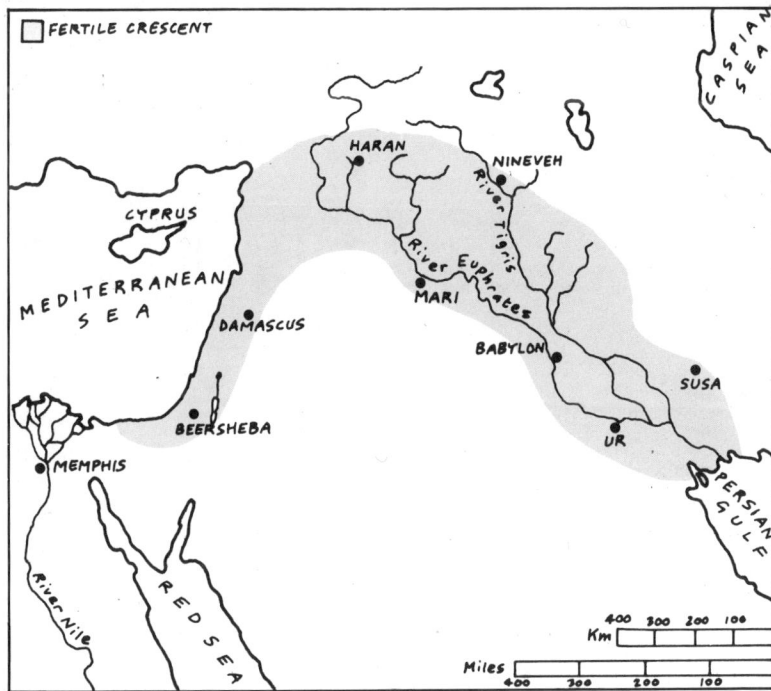

480 CLAY TABLETS
(54.5 kg / 120 lbs)

1 PAPERBACK
(85 gms / 3 ozs)

1 DISK
(14 gms / ½ oz)

Reading a novel in ancient times could have been heavy work. You would need 480 clay tablets to contain all the words in a single 144-page paperback. Today, one computer disk would take all the words.

THE FERTILE CRESCENT

Abraham was a man who lived in an area called the Fertile Crescent around 1900 BC. This area was shaped like a semi-circle and represented fertile land which surrounded the great rivers of the Tigris and the Euphrates.

ORIGINAL PICTOGRAPH	EARLY BABYLONIAN	ASSYRIAN	ORIGINAL MEANING
			BIRD
			ORCHARD

The earliest writing used pictures, but *cuneiform* writing was more advanced. Wedged-shaped sticks were used to make impressions into clay, which was then baked hard. Everything was written in this way in the area of the Fertile Crescent – legal documents, accounts of battles, and even letters, which came in their own clay envelope.

UR

Abraham lived at Ur. In 1900 BC Ur was already an ancient and civilized city. At the time of Abraham it had well-made houses to suit the climate, and a good drainage system. The people wrote on clay tablets, many of which have been found by archaeologists. These are known as cuneiform tablets, and they tell us that highly developed trade brought prosperity to the city. People worshipped the moon God (named Nannar or Sin) and built a great temple tower called a Ziggurat. Here is one which has been partially re-constructed.

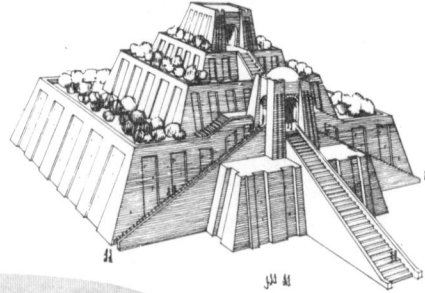

·F·O·L·L·O·W·U·P·

1. Draw the map of the Fertile Crescent and label all the towns, rivers and seas..

2. Copy the example of cuneiform and write a paragraph on how it was done.

3. Moon worship. The Ziggurat at Ur was seventy feet high, 200 feet long and 150 feet wide. It had three terraces to the temple of the moon god, which was at the top of a long stone staircase. The ziggurat was also used by the priests for the study of the stars. They believed that the positions of planets and star formations were signs from the gods of what would happen in the future. We call this astrology (*not* astronomy)
Draw the ziggurat at Ur.

God Calls Abraham

DESERT SUN

25 January, 1900 BC

ABEY BABY LEAVES TOWN FOR MYSTERY TOUR

Rich farmer Abram and his beautiful but childless wife Sarai left Haran yesterday with cattle, sheep, goats and slaves to start a new life – the only trouble is, they don't know where they're going!

Abram (Abey Baby to his friends) and his family moved here some thirty years ago, when his father Terah left the razzle-dazzle living of downtown Ur, the metropolis of the South, to enjoy his retirement in the country. Since then Abe has been all the rave!

His last year's design for an air-conditioned Ziggurat won him acclaim as 'Abe the cool, he's nobody's fool'. This, plus an ingenious new project, 'The collapsible tent for Mesopotamian nomads in the know', has led to the building of four Rent-A-Tent centres in the Euphrates shopping centre. Abe is not one to be pegged down! Imagine, therefore, our surprise when we got wind of his imminent departure.

MYSTERY

Our reporter Keepya Aaron rushed to Abram's house to find this frisky 75 year old ready for the off. He refused to give a formal interview but was heard muttering: 'Well, well, I'll be a grandad yet'.

Friends say that lately Abram has been missing moon worship

and child sacrifice times. Instead he has been spotted wandering alone in the fields. One farmer thought he spotted Abram talking aloud to himself. The reason for his sudden move from fame, fortune and a luxurious apartment at No. 7 Fertile Crescent to a wandering existence in sticky tents surrounded by locusts and bad-tempered camels remains a mystery. What makes a man do such a thing? We'd like to hear your answers.

Send your clay tablets to the Editor.

TODAY
in your soaraway
SUN

page 3
Miss Mesopotamia

page 5
Camel Racing

page 22
Your Stars

BINGO!

Check your number on the clay tablet enclosed

ABRAHAM'S FAMILY TREE

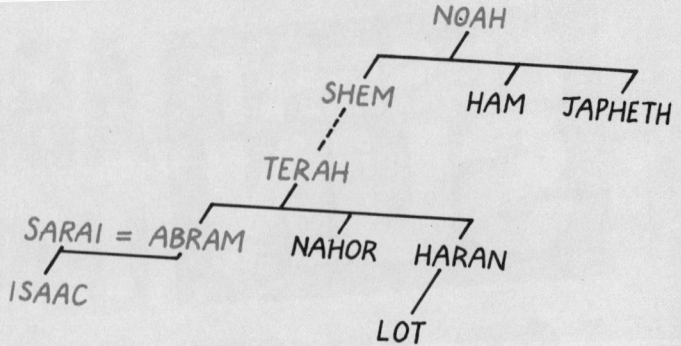

NOAH

SHEM   HAM   JAPHETH

TERAH

SARAI = ABRAM   NAHOR   HARAN

ISAAC

LOT

·F·O·L·L·O·W·U·P·

1. General knowledge. Answer these questions:
● Who was Abram's father?
● Who was Abram's wife?
● What was God's instruction to Abram?
● Name three things that God promised him.
● What was Abram's response to God's call?

2. People today still talk about 'a call' to do certain things. Some jobs are classified by the word 'vocation', a word that literally means 'call'. Usually the sort of work that is vocational includes a large degree of self-sacrifice on behalf of others and therefore it includes commitment to a cause or to people in need. What sort of work do you think is vocational? Choose three of the following and say why you think it is a 'vocation'.

Postman	Working with
Nurse/Male Nurse	mentally ill
Dish-Washer	Typist
Missionary	Footballer
Shop Assistant	Miner
Member of	Car factory worker
Parliament	Florist
Teacher	Hotel Receptionist
Trainee mechanic	Ambulance driver
Fireman	or helper
Surgeon	Policeman/
	Policewoman

ABRAM HEARS GOD

Abram's family had moved from the highly civilized Ur to another city, Haran, in the north. But Abram left the comforts of Haran to become a nomad, setting out for an unknown destination.

Although everyone worshipped the moon-god, Abram discovered a God who spoke to him. God said 'Leave!' and Abram left! We don't know whether he heard God speak to him directly in words, in his thoughts, in a vision, or what, but Abram was so convinced that he upped tools and went, taking his family with him. This is how the Bible describes Abram's call:

I'VE COME FOR PART 2 OF THE LORD OF THE RINGS!

CUNEIFORM LIBRARY

'The Lord said to Abram, "Leave your native land, your relatives and your father's home and go to a country that I am going to show you. I will give you many descendants and they will become a great nation. I will bless you and make your name famous so that you will be a blessing. I will bless those who bless you but I will curse those who curse you, and through you I will bless all the nations."'

'When Abram was 75 years old he started out from Haran as the Lord had told him to do, and Lot went with him. Abram took his wife Sarai, his nephew Lot and all the wealth and all the slaves they had acquired in Haran and they started out for the land of Canaan.'

Genesis, Chapter 12

God's Agreement with Abraham

A 'COVENANT' IS AN AGREEMENT OR PROMISE.

In this covenant with Abram, God took the first step to have a relationship with people once again. It would have been very easy for Abram to ignore God speaking to him. There would have been plenty of excuses. No one else believed in a God like this, and what would his friends think? But Abram believed that it was God speaking to him. He had faith.

Genesis chapter 15, verse 6 says: 'Abraham put his trust in the Lord and because of this, the Lord was pleased with him and accepted him.' Abram must have had faith! God asked him to believe that he would have thousands of descendants, even though he and his wife were both childless in their old age.

Faith and trust go together. If I trust you, I have faith in you that you will not do anything intended to hurt me. I may have no evidence that you won't let me down, but somehow I believe

> *PSSST! BY THE WAY, READERS, ABRAHAM WAS EARLIER KNOWN AS ABRAM. SO DON'T WORRY ABOUT THE CHANGE IN SPELLING...*

The 19th century tightrope walker, L'Estrange. Someone might believe that they can walk on a high-wire, but doing it is the important thing. For Christians, faith is a matter of doing what you believe in.

in *you* as a person. We are pleased when people trust us and usually we want to live up to their trust. God was pleased with Abram's trust in him so he confirmed his promise by ritual and a sign.

THE COVENANT RITUAL

A ritual is a religious act; often one that is repeated on different occasions. In the days of Abram people would kill and divide certain animals to make it clear that if anybody broke the promise or the agreement, the penalty was death. It was like a kind of oath. So Abram killed some animals. But in this story it is only God who puts himself on oath by passing between the pieces of meat. You can read it in Genesis chapter 15. Obviously, a promise was meant to be kept!

THE COVENANT SIGN

We still use signs as a means of identification and status. A gold ring on a man or woman's third finger usually signifies that they are married. A large red cross on a van means that medical aid is available. God gave Abram a sign, the sign of circumcision.

Circumcision is a minor operation to cut away the loose skin covering the end of the penis. It was performed on a baby boy on the eighth day after his birth. When God promised Abram that he would be the founder of a great nation, the nation of Israel, he commanded that all his male descendants should be circumcised. This was to be the physical sign that they were the people of God. Today, almost 4000 years later, Abraham's covenant sign is still given to newborn Jewish babies.

NEW NAMES

God gave Abram the new name 'Abraham', which means something like 'father of many nations' in Hebrew. Sarai's name was also changed to Sarah. When she was very old she bore a son, Isaac.

Later God tested Abraham's faith when he was told to kill

GOD'S AGREEMENT WITH ABRAHAM

GOD'S PROMISE	THE PROMISE FULFILLED
A land/country	Canaan (later called Israel)
Many descendants that would become a great nation	All who put their trust in God
God's blessing	He had friendship with God
A name that is famous	We are still learning about him. For Jewish and Muslim people he is specially famous
Through Abraham all the world would be blessed	Not only Jewish people have their identity through him, but Christians all over the world have entered into the heritage of faith.

WHO HAS THE MOST FAITH?

Isaac and offer him to God. When God stopped Abraham from doing this at the last possible moment, it was to show that he did not want child sacrifice as did all the 'gods' of that time – but he did want to test Abraham's loyalty and obedience to him.

GOD'S FRIEND

In Genesis chapter 1, Adam and Eve chose to rule themselves and go their own way. In Genesis chapter 12, Abram chose God's way and became his friend.

·F·O·L·L·O·W·U·P·

1. Find and read these other stories of Abraham in the Bible:
God promises Abraham a son
Genesis 15:1–6
God tests Abraham's faith
Genesis 22
Abraham pleads for Sodom
Genesis 18:16–32

2. New words: Explain what is meant by:
● Covenant   ● Archaeologist
● Nomad   ● Faith
● Excavate

3. Faith and trust are things we have to use daily in one way or another, but we usually do it without thinking. We trust that there's going to be food for us. We trust that the laws of gravity will not suddenly change and throw us about. This is using faith in a very weak way, for there is hardly any effort on our part. We *assume* that because things have happened so far, they will continue to happen in the same way. But sometimes our faith and trust has to be stretched. What about if we go into hospital for a major operation? We have to have faith in the surgeon and it's usually someone we don't know who has our life in his or her hands.

Give three examples of situations in which you have to exercise your faith a lot.

4. Discuss who is having the most faith in the cartoon pictures.

Bringing People Together

'I, John, take you, Susan,
to be my wife,
to have and to hold
from this day forward;
for better, for worse,
for richer, for poorer,
in sickness and in health,
to love and to cherish,
till death us do part,
according to God's holy law;
and this is my solemn vow.'

Wedding Vows

HUSBAND AND WIFE AGREEMENTS

People are joined in marriage when they publicly commit themselves to live together for life, and to be faithful to each other. This agreement is made before someone in authority (a registrar or church minister) and is usually witnessed by friends and relations.

From the left, Winston Churchill, President Roosevelt and Josef Stalin meet at Yalta in February 1945, during World War II. They met as the allies (Britain, the United States, Russia) fighting against Hitler. But the alliance quickly fell apart after the war.

Marriage in more than three quarters of the world means that a man or a woman has only one marriage partner. This marriage structure is called *monogamy* – one partner. But there are other alternatives. *Polygamy* is where one man has several wives. *Polyandry* is where one woman has several husbands. Muslims have traditionally practised polygamy, although not so many do so today.

In all marriages of whatever sort there is an agreement between the partners that gives them both legal status and rights. To be married, it is not enough to love one another. What makes you married is the public commitment you have made to one another. This is in the presence of witnesses and involves a promise: 'And this is my solemn vow'. The sign of the agreement is then given, as the ring is placed on the bride's finger (and often on the groom's, too).

The couple have made a covenant with each other – mutual promises have been exchanged and the responsibility for the marriage being a success depends on both the man and the woman and their level of commitment to each other.

PACTS AND TREATIES

Sometimes agreements are made between nations. If you look through history books, you would find countless examples of pacts which were made as promises of peace between different countries. It is difficult enough for promises to be kept between two people, let alone between two whole nations! There are always groups within a country who disagree with the policy of its leaders. So a legal document called a 'treaty' is signed. This is the sign of the agreement. Treaties can be about all sorts of things: boundaries of territory, limitation of ammunition and arms, trade routes, and many other agreements. There can be dire consequences if the treaty is broken.

A TREATY WITH GOD

The word 'covenant' (meaning 'agreement') is used nearly 300 times in the Old Testament. Sometimes it means two tribes making a treaty. Sometimes it means two people making friends. But mostly it means the agreement between the Israelite people and their God. The most important covenant in the Old Testament is the covenant God made with the nation of Israel on Mt Sinai in the time of Moses.

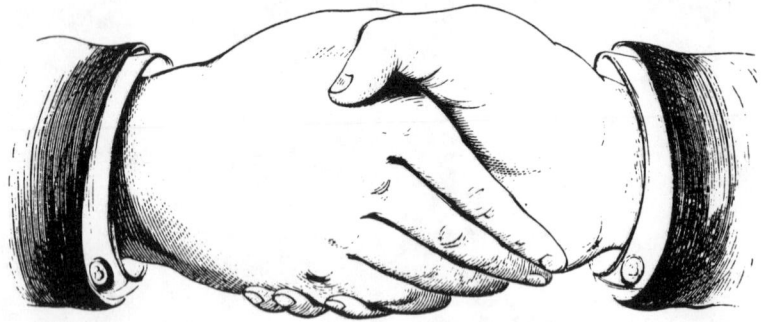

F·O·L·L·O·W·U·P·

1. The promises made by people in marriage are difficult to keep even if both parties love one another. There are days when the 'feelings' disappear beneath the problems, and it takes a lot of determination to carry on until things get better. In your opinion which of the following contribute most to promises being broken in marriage? Do you think there are ways in which these sorts of pressures can be avoided?
○ Lack of money
○ Annoying habits
○ Poor housing, or living with parents
○ Responsibility of a baby early in the marriage
○ Very few common interests
○ One partner falls in love with someone else

○ Hurtful things said in arguments and no apologies made

2. 'Are promises important?' Write a page using this title, and say why you think promises are important or not so important. Include any incident you may know of where promises have been broken either between friends or others. Were the consequences good or bad?

The Moses Connection

THE STORY SO FAR . . .

In case you feel lost, the story in Genesis happened something like this:

God creates the world and mankind and all that he makes is good. He gives man and woman the choice to follow him or not.

Adam and Eve (representing mankind) turn away from God and choose self-rule. They lose their close friendship with God.

God renews his friendship with people and he chooses Abraham to be his friend. God's covenant with Abraham is that he will be the founder of a great nation who will belong to God.

God sends a great flood to prevent human evil from growing worse, but he saves Noah who is said to be good. God makes an agreement with Noah, promising never again to flood the earth. A rainbow is the sign of God's agreement.

Self-rule (sin) becomes characteristic of mankind. The first murder is committed (read the story of Cain and Abel in Genesis chapter 4) and wickedness begins to spread.

Years later, Joseph, Abraham's great-grandson, is sold as a slave by his brothers when he is 17 years old. He is then taken to Egypt. Eventually he rises in power from prisoner to Prime Minister because God is with him. Joseph is told by God to store up grain as famine is coming. In time his brothers travel from Canaan to Egypt in search of food. They are unable to recognize the rich ruler as their own brother (read Genesis chapters 42–47 for the astonishing story).

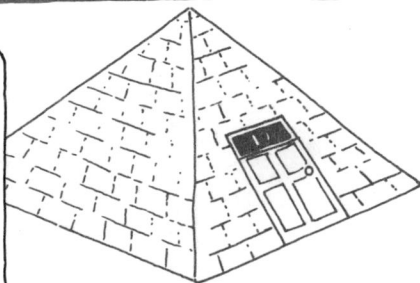

Eventually Joseph's whole family settle in Egypt. They have moved from Canaan, the land which God gave them.

Four hundred years later, Joseph's descendants (now an enormous number of people) have become slaves of the Egyptians.

God calls Moses to lead the people out of slavery. After a series of dramatic events, the Israelites (as they are now called) escape and travel to Mt Sinai. Here, God makes a covenant with them.

GOD'S INSTRUCTIONS

It was not Moses' idea to make a friendship with God. It was God's idea. God offered his friendship to the Israelites and Moses accepted it. (You can read all about it in Exodus chapter 3.) As the leader, Moses went up to Mt Sinai and the people camped at the bottom. There amid smoke and thunder the Lord spoke and gave Moses his instructions regarding duty to himself and duty to other people.

DUTY · TO · GOD

~1~
DO NOT WORSHIP OTHER GODS

~2~
DO NOT MAKE IDOLS

~3~
DO NOT TAKE GOD'S NAME IN VAIN

~4~
KEEP ONE DAY A WEEK FOR A REST

~5~
HONOUR YOUR PARENTS

DUTY · TO · OTHERS

~6~
DO NOT COMMIT MURDER

~7~
DO NOT COMMIT ADULTERY

~8~
DO NOT STEAL

~9~
DO NOT TELL LIES ABOUT OTHERS

~10~
DO NOT BE JEALOUS OF WHAT ANOTHER MAN HAS.

THE COVENANT RITUAL

A special ceremony was held. Moses built an altar and also twelve pillars to represent the twelve tribes of Israel which were descended from the twelve sons of Jacob. Then animals were sacrificed. Half the blood was thrown upon the altar, and the rest of the blood was put into basins.

THE COVENANT SIGN

The blood in the basins was then thrown by Moses on to the people and he said, 'This is the blood that seals the covenant which the Lord made with you when he gave all these commands.'

We have mentioned already that shedding blood was a sign of the seriousness of the promise, representing death. Even today, when people are trying to show how serious they are about something, they say 'Cross my heart and hope to die'. This oath is an attempt to show how serious they are.

In this covenant at Mt Sinai, the response of the people is very important. God doesn't say, 'Unless you do this, I won't offer my friendship to you,' but it is obvious that unless the people obey him then their friendship can't work as it should and the covenant is broken.

The Jewish High Priest offered sacrifices to God for the sins of the people. He came before God on behalf of all the people. The twelve precious stones on his breastplate represented the twelve tribes of ancient Israel.

SACRIFICE

The Israelites sacrificed animals and the blood was collected into a bowl. One half of the blood was sprinkled over the worshippers and the other half would be burnt on the altar. In this way the person performing the sacrifice thought the animal was dying in his place – or instead of him. The blood was the animal's 'life', so its life was taken because sin had been committed – and the penalty for sin was death. As the Israelites offered sacrifices, the animal acted as a substitute for them.

This idea of a 'substitute' is seen more clearly in the idea of choosing a particular goat. On the day called the Day of Atonement, the sins of the people were symbolically placed on the goat, and it was then driven away into the desert to die. 'Atonement' means covering, so during this day the sins of all the people were thought to have been covered over by God.

F·O·L·L·O·W·U·P·

1. Sacrifice is to do with life being given up. In ancient days this was literally to do with blood and death. In what ways today do men and women give up their lives for what they believe is right?

2. You can tell a lot about people by what they say. What do God's laws tell you about what God is like?

59

The Jesus Connection

DECEMBER
13 Monday   198_
                                                 Week 50

Last week of term!

   Dentist 4.30 p.m. Aaaargh!

14 Tuesday

Party at Sue's 8 p.m.
Jane was there, I danced with
her, but Richard got to walk her
home. Great!

15 Wednesday ●

7 p.m. Youth Club. Lift?

16 Thursday

Richard asked me if he could borrow
£20 from my savings for Xmas. He's
short of cash. Made him write out
an I.O.U. as a joke! MUST
remember to get him
to pay it back!!

I.O.U.

FROM   Richard.

TO   Geoff.

I.O.U. £20.

SIGNED (in blood!) [blue]

16th December.

P.S. If I don't pay, or die before
I pay, you can have my
record collection!

THIS
WAY!

Thursday 20 January

Went to the Post Office to take
out some money, but I only had
£2.51 in there. So I called in on
Richard. He didn't mention the
money, so after a couple of hours
I reminded him that he owed me
£20.
   He got a bit angry and said
that he couldn't yet afford to
pay me back. After we'd argued
a bit he promised to pay it all
back at the end of the month. I
left just after that as he
wanted to watch Eastenders.
I don't like arguing with
friends, but I do need the
money...

PASS TO RICHARD

Sorry to disturb you during the
world's most boring double maths.
It's 6th March today. You promised
to give me back my £20 by the end
of January. I want to stay
friends, but I also want my cash!
Do you want me to come + get
your record collection or are
you gonna pay up?
Geoff

re-arrange this

well known phrase or

saying: OFF NAFF.
                          Richard.

Friday 6 May

For the 1st time for a couple of months, Richard + I talked today, near the football pitch. We didn't talk about the £20, because I deliberately didn't bring it up, and so we got on O.K. It was like old times again.

But even when we were laughing at a joke he told, I felt cheated. He still owes me the money, he <u>hasn't</u> paid me, and it <u>doesn't</u> seem to worry him.

Nothing's really sorted out at all — and yet I want him as a friend. What should I do?

Geoff, having a great time here, doing nothing all day, spending lotsa money trying to stay out of my mums + dads clutches. Sea's warm so we're swimming all day and there are plenty of discos etc, at night. We come back this Saturday. I've bought a £35 camera out here, so you can see my pix when I get back home — just to make you envious!

June 21st.

Richard.

COSTA LOT, MAJORCA

GEOFF WALKER
3, THE GABLES.
SOUTH FIELDS ROAD.
EAST HILL
LONDON.
ENGLAND.

THIS WAY

Monday 18 July

Richard came round today with his photos of Majorca (taken with the camera that <u>I</u> paid £20 towards. It was all I could do not to hit him. We had a good talk, though. Mum and Dad have been down on me since last week and it was good to talk about it with Richard — he knew what it was like.

I've thought about it a lot + I've decided to forget about the £20 he owes me — I'd rather have him as a friend. After all, it's only money! (Even if it is £20.)

Tuesday 19th July

Dear Richard,

Please accept the £20 I lent you last December as a present from me. Forget about paying it back — it's yours.

Your friend,

Geoff

P.S. I've torn up the I.O.U!

GOD DOESN'T GIVE UP

In the Bible, God is like the good friend in this story. He makes an agreement with Israel, but it is broken. He tries again and again – sometimes the people respond to him, but eventually he is ignored. The covenant with the nation through Moses was ignored as time went on and God sent prophets (men who spoke out for him) to tell the people that God would forgive them if they would only recognize their selfishness and return to him. Either they wouldn't, or, like the friend in the story, they couldn't because they had got to the point where they didn't care about God.

They still worshipped God, but only with words. Inside they went their own way refusing to keep his laws. But still God didn't give up. Like the good friend in the story, God's love for his people was genuine and persistent. Seven hundred years after the time of Moses, the prophet Jeremiah spoke out what was on God's mind. He told them that God would do a new thing.

WHAT JEREMIAH SAID . . .

GOD'S NEW AGREEMENT

Christians believe that what Jeremiah wrote was fulfilled 600 years later in the life and death of Jesus Christ. The New Testament explains that Jesus made a new agreement between God and the human race, so that people could become his friends again. But what was so special about Jesus that he could do this? Christians believe that he was ideally suited, because . . .
● He was uniquely God's own Son – a human being as we are, and yet also God living on Earth.
● Although he was tempted as everyone is to do wrong, he never gave in. He was the only perfect person ever.
● Jesus died a criminal's death although he had done nothing to deserve it. He did this to show the extent of God's love for the human race and to bring people back to God.
● Jesus was raised from death and appeared to his followers alive again to show that evil and death had been defeated.

The time is coming when I will make a new covenant with the people of Israel and with the people of Judah. It will not be like the old covenant that I made with their ancestors when I took them by the hand and led them out of Egypt. Although I was like a husband to them, they did not keep that covenant. The new covenant that I will make with the people of Israel will be this: I will put my law within them and write it on their hearts. I will be their God and they will be my people. None of them will have to teach his fellow-countryman to know the Lord, because all will know me from the least to the greatest. I will forgive their sins and I will no longer remember their wrongs. I the Lord have spoken.'

But how did Jesus' death repair the broken friendship between people and God? Several pictures in the Bible explain it.

GOD'S PART OF THE AGREEMENT

● **SUBSTITUTE** Because he was perfect, Jesus could be the representative or substitute for people as the spotless goat was in the Old Testament. Just as the sins of the people were symbolically placed on the animal and then its life was offered instead of their own, so now the sins of the world are placed on Jesus and his life is offered on behalf of the human race. He 'carries the can', for everyone. People deserve death for breaking the promise – but he dies for them.

● **SAVIOUR** A saviour is someone who saves somebody else from danger and death. Jesus' own explanation of his death was that he was giving himself as a ransom payment. Today, a ransom is the money demanded by kidnappers or terrorist groups as the condition on which they release a prisoner. In Jesus' day the ransom was a price paid to secure the freedom of a slave. Jesus took this idea to show that his life was a payment to secure the freedom of men and women from the slavery of sin and the terrorism of death and the horror of being cut off from the meaning of life. The result is that people who accept God's gift of life have a new owner – God himself.

● **EXAMPLE** Jesus' death and his life are an example of how to face and endure injustice and how Christians can live in the world. He not only taught about the life God wants people to lead, he actually lived it out, and *showed* what God was like.

GOD'S AGREEMENTS: TWO-WAY PROMISES

Covenant with	Bible reference	God's promise	Human response	The sign
Noah	Genesis 6	God will never again flood the earth and destroy it.		Rainbow
Abraham	Genesis 12, 15 and 17	You will be the father of a great nation, I will give you a land to live in.	Faith in God	Circumcision
Nation of Israel, through Moses	Exodus 20 and 24	I will be your God, you will be my people.	Obey the law of the Lord	Sacrifices
King David	2 Samuel 7	I will make your name famous. I will keep you safe from your enemies. You will always have descendants. Your kingdom will last forever.		
Nation of Israel, through Ezekiel and Jeremiah	Ezekiel 37:26 Jeremiah 31:31	I will give you a new heart and a new mind. I will put my spirit within you.	Shame and honesty about their sins	
Christian believers, through Jesus of Nazareth	Luke 22: 19–20 Matthew 26: 26–28	'This is my blood which seals God's covenant, my blood poured out for many for the forgiveness of sins.'	Faith in God's gift of Jesus	Wine and bread at the communion service

·F·O·L·L·O·W·U·P·

1. Jesus suffered pain and death and Christians believe it was to show people how much the world matters to God. Here are some things other people have suffered for:
● To end slavery and the slave trade
● To fight for women's rights and equality
● To abolish nuclear weapons
● To improve working conditions for children
● To protect their country from foreign occupation
Is there anything you would be prepared to suffer for?

2. Read the story about the good friend at the beginning of this unit. What do you think of the friend who forgave? Is he a fool? Or is he someone you would like to have as a friend? What would you have done in his situation?

3. Read the events recorded in the Bible about Jesus' arrest, trial, mugging and eventual suffering and death on the cross.
The arrest – Matthew 26: 47–56
His trial by the Council – Matthew 26: 56–67
His trial by the Romans – Matthew 27: 11–26
Jesus is mugged – Matthew 27: 27–31
Jesus is crucified – Matthew 27: 32–56

4. Try to find out (for example, from a local church) how the communion service, mass or eucharist is a vivid visual aid to involve the believer in the death of Jesus for sin. Names for the service vary; so do the churches in the emphasis they put upon it. Can you find out what the main emphasis is of a church near you?

PEOPLE'S RESPONSE TO GOD'S AGREEMEN

Christians are people who have accepted God's agreement through Jesus, and who have became God's friends again. Often Christians get excited about Jesus because he shows them just how much love God must have for them if he went to such lengths as sacrificing his own Son for the world. Because of this they want to please God in return. They commit themselves to going God's way instead of their own. They do this not only because they *have* to, but because they *want* to. There is a new spirit within them, God's Spirit, and so the prophet Jeremiah's words come true for everyone who accepts God's covenant in Jesus:

'I will put my law within them; they shall be my people and I will be their God.'